Written, edited and designed by the editorial staff of ORTHO Books.

Basic research and manuscript:
Leavitt Dudley

Weather consultant:
John H. Aldrich
Certified Consulting Meteorologist

Coordinator of University Experiment
Station Information:
Dr. John W. Courter, Extension
Specialist
University of Illinois

Special consultants:
A. Cort Sinnes
James K. McNair

# Weather-Wise Gardening

## Contents

# How's your weather?

Your house and whatever outside space that surrounds it—be it a small enclosed patio, or an acre sized yard—is your own personal environment. While technology hasn't brought us to the point where we can do anything about the overall climate of an area, your own house and yard will yield to a number of modifications that can make your living and gardening more comfortable and successful both inside and out.

Whether you've moved into a new house with nothing surrounding it but bare ground, or are living in a house whose surrounding yard was landscaped years ago, thoughtful planning and planting (or pruning) will result in advantages that nature, or the building contractor neglected to give.

Well planned landscaping can create a wealth of new comfort zones for you and your plants, and better the indoor climate of your home at the same time. Each tree and shrub changes the conditions around it. Every alteration, fence, patio, or walkway will have some effect on the small-sized climate which surrounds your home.

Vegetables and other plants, whose native climate was much different from that of your yard can be grown side by side in the garden. New developments in plant breeding, various mulches, new methods of irrigation and ways to increase or decrease the power of the sun, all help to modify the growing climate for better vegetables and more bountiful crops.

Our grandparents bettered their living through the use of microclimatic principles because they had to. They couldn't count on central heating and air conditioning to regulate the climates of their homes. Most of the methods of control are the same now as they were then, needing only a bit of effort and ingenuity to put them to work.

The weatherwise gardener is both observant and ingenious. He can make the most of his climate by keeping a close watch on the weather and the individual conditions around his yard. He knows that he cannot make a poor climate perfect, but through modification he can certainly improve it.

*Shade trees establish small microclimate areas throughout the general landscape.*

*Plastic Garden at Dixon Springs Agricultural Center in Simpson, Illinois, combines flowers and vegetables mulched with black plastic. Sawdust used between rows.*

*Grapes trained to grow all around the house are not only beautiful, but effective in climate control and provide a bountiful harvest annually.*

*Thoughtful planting can create an "oasis" for the gardener. This one includes plantings along a ventilated fence that moderates the air flow and provides privacy.*

If you have lived in any one place for a number of years you begin to know the climate of your yard on a familiar basis. You've probably found out that a plant that thrives on the north side of the house would wither and die on the south side And, except in years of extreme weather conditions, the familiar patterns of growth appear season after season. Certain signs signal the change of seasons and the observant gardener responds accordingly.

Just to be in a garden through the seasons is an experience full of wonders.

There's the miracle of renewal—new shoots poking through soil that yesterday was lifeless. There's the feel and smell of the rushing, throbbing growth of early spring.

There are the ever-changing kinds of light: the cool green dancing light through the leafy screen of a young birch beyond the bedroom window; the tinted afternoon sunlight sifting through the foliage of a purple-leafed plum; the low, warm, red light from the setting summer sun, signaling the cool of the evening, giving you a shadow 30 feet long, transforming your scraggly lawn into a rich, dark-green carpet. And there's the restful beauty of the garden's slow retreat into winter.

But the pleasures of life in the garden grow richer as you observe how the plants grow and move in step with the cycle of the seasons.

Weatherwise gardeners attempt to make the most out of each season. They realize that the relationship between man and plants is a congenial one. If the gardener provides the best possible growing environment for the plant, the plant responds by improving the environment for man. It is our hope that this book will provide the necessary practical information that will result in a better environment for all.

# Folklore: facts or fiction?

Farmers and other weather watchers have sworn by certain signs, conditions and feelings through the years to predict natural phenomena. Some of the early prophetic legends have fallen by the wayside or proved erroneous over the years, but in many instances the time-honored tests seem to be surprisingly accurate.

The reactions of birds, insects, animals, and plants to changing atmospherics has long been used to

forecast the weather, however, Indian tribes and pioneer European settlers were often quite accurate in their predictions, though the immigrants were puzzled for a time by the unfamiliar varieties of the new continent's climates.

Later, early Americans compiled their findings into "almanacks," and based the year-long forecasts upon moon positions. Their conclusions were as scientific as anything else at the time, and many hold good today.

Pioneers benefited from the natural climatic instincts of wildlife. For instance:

"Observe the way the hedgehog
     builds her nest,
To front the north or south or east
     or west;
For if 'tis true what common peo-
     ple say,
The wind will blow the quite con-
     trary way."
This observation helped in the orientation of pioneer homes.
"A cow with its tail to the west,
     makes weather the best;
A cow with its tail to the east,
     makes weather the least."

Animals graze tail to the wind, a natural instinct to face and see a predator. The invader would not approach from the opposite direction as wind would carry its scent to its victim. As an easterly in the colonies was a rain wind and the westerly brought fair skies, the cow's tail was a weather indicator.

"Raining cats and dogs" is a contraction and mispronunciation of a Pennsylvania German saying, "It is raining to keep in the cats and bring out the ducks."

Birds provided several clues to the weather ahead, then and now. Generally speaking, they roost more during a low pressure period preceding a storm because thinner air makes flying more difficult than in the dense air of a high.

High pressure also raises the altitude levels of migrating flights, and indicated fair weather, while a lower flight meant low pressure.

"South or north, sally forth; West or east, travel least" referred to the migration of geese. When the flock flew on an even course, fair weather was ahead. If it deflected east or west to detour a storm ahead, the next day would bring unsettled weather.

Swallows and bats flew close to the ground before a rain because of their delicate hearing mechanisms.

Sensitive to a sudden pressure drop, they skimmed the ground to take advantage of the densest air level.

Gliding birds indicated unstable air and later showers, as they rode rising currents rather than flapping their wings.

Crickets were amazingly accurate weather instruments, responding to temperature changes faster than a thermometer. They chirp faster when warm than cold. The number of chirps in 14 seconds, plus 40, gives the temperature of their locations.

The furry woolly bear caterpillar has a brown center stripe bordered by black on both ends. The wider this middle band, the milder the winter would be. No one knew the reason for this, and it's still a mystery.

Plants foretold the weather in different ways.

"When the forest murmurs and the mountain roars" indicated a cold-front storm was at hand. The wind starts at high altitude and descends to earth, so the trees were only stirring to a changed air current while the mountain tops already felt its full force.

"When the leaves show their backs, it will rain." Leaves grow according to prevailing winds. During a non-prevailing storm wind, they are ruffled backward and show their undersides.

Milkweed, dandelions, clover, and some other plants change their leaf attitude with increasing humidity which sometimes indicated rain to pioneers. Laurel and rhododendron close theirs as the air becomes colder.

Settlers actually "heard bad weather approaching" by the hollow sounds from faraway sources, which predicted a long rain from a warm front storm under stable air and a temperature inversion. In Old Testament times Elijah "heard the sound of abundance of rain."

The chimney was a common weather indicator by its sounds, the way the wood burned, and the action of the smoke, giving rise to the sayings "A storm makes its first announcement down the chimney," or "A storm wind settles in the chimney, but a clear wind coaxes out its smoke."

Early American noses were able to predict stormy weather by smell. Odors held to the ground by high pressure in ditches, swamps, and low areas were released in low pressure, thus the proverb "When ditches and cellars smell most, a long rain is near."

Discomforts of unfortunates afflicted with corns, stiff joints, tooth-aches, or other maladies felt the weather as lowering air pressure intensified their pains. One of our trained meteorologists personally believes such pains are good indicators, but are due to a positive *ion* charge near the ground, as before a thunderstorm, rather than to air pressure. The *ions* provide good nuclei to raindrops.

Settlers were careful, as we are

today, to eat oysters only during months containing an R. Other months are warm enough that bivalves (two valved shell animals) may harbor sewage germs. The colder water in the "R" period descends and lifts debris to the surface out of their reach.

A fishing proverb said: "When the wind is in the north, The skillful fisher goes not forth; When the wind is from the south, It blows the fly in the fish's mouth." Which may have some truth to it, as the lines were written by the patron saint of fisher-men, Izaak Walton.

Though we are better insulated from the weather and less sensitive to its changing conditions, its periods still affect our own behavior and attitudes.

Benjamin Franklin advised long ago that we "do business with men when the wind is in the northwest," where the atmosphere is more likely to be dry and pleasant. In a low pressure depression, dejection and irritability are more common.

Tempers can surface more quickly in periods of dry heat, particularly during the strong downslope winds when the weather is as hard on us as it is on our plants.

# The world in your vegetable garden

When you stop and think about it, a vegetable garden is quite an amazing accomplishment. There, in a small area, are vegetables from all over the world, vegetables whose native climates were quite dissimilar: peppers from the Caribbean, tomatoes from South America, cucumbers from India, and lettuce from the Mediterranean and the Near East. It is something of a wonder how these and other vegetables can grow successfully, side by side, in your own back yard.

If a gardener grew only those vegetables which were native to his area, his vegetable garden would be very limited in variety. The general climate, the temperature, the rainfall, the day length of a certain area limits the number of plants which grow there naturally. Compensating for a plant's limitations is up to the plant breeders; compensating for the climate is up to the gardener.

Each plant, whether vegetable or ornamental, has certain genetic limitations. The plant's limitations govern how it reacts in various climates. Humans have the same kind of genetic limitations which limit the type of environment we can survive and grow in. If the temperature around us gets too hot or too cold we complain—if the temperature continues into the extremes, we stop living; the same thing holds true for plants.

Plant breeders continually work to develop new varieties and hybrids which are more tolerant to climatic conditions. They also work to develop varieties which are resistant to the diseases of a particular area. If you have had trouble growing cucumbers, tomatoes or other vegetables bothered by diseases be sure and take advantage of the breeder's success and choose disease resistant varieties at planting time.

The progress which plant breeders have made is one of the primary reasons gardeners can grow such a wide variety of plants, vegetables and otherwise, in their yards.

The home gardener can take up where the plant breeder leaves off. In this next chapter we've looked at some of the methods, modifications and ideas that university test stations and weather-wise gardeners have developed.

*Even the common varieties of vegetables grown in the home garden have diverse original climates: Left, top to bottom: Lettuce from the Mediterranean, eggplant from India, tomatoes from South America, cucumbers from India. Right, top to bottom: Kohlrabi from northern Europe, cabbage from central Europe, beans from Central America, peppers from the Caribbean, and carrots from the Mediterranean.*

# Making the most out of what you have

A gardener doesn't really grow a plant—a plant grows by itself, and it is up to the gardener to see that it has the right kind of environment to grow in. A plant's environment includes the soil, water, sunlight, temperature and food it receives.

By its very nature, a plant wants to grow—if it doesn't grow chances are that the gardener failed to provide the right environment for the plant.

This chapter looks at home gardeners and university researchers who are bent upon making plants grow; providing the best possible environment for the best possible results; for the most part they are "weatherwise gardeners." If their climate is deficient in some way they modify it to better suit the plant's needs.

Changing the natural climate to protect or further the growth of vegetables is one of the most rewarding exercises in gardening. In this endeavor the resourcefulness of gardeners is astounding. The good gardeners who contribute their good ideas for vegetable production and protection on these next pages prove the point.

How can the temperature level be raised? Some additional gain can be made by planting warm-season crops just south of a tall reflective surface such as a tall fence, or a row of corn or sunflowers. Planting on the south side of a ridge increases heat for young plants.

Plastic cottage cheese containers and the like from the market, and plastic jugs with the bottoms removed (see warning page 21) are used in many ways for the early protection of seedlings.

Modifying a plant's growing climate takes other forms too. University researchers and commercial growers (not to mention a few fearless home gardeners) have worked with polyethylene film used as a mulch. Both clear and black plastic are efficient temperature changers. The use of polyethylene as a mulch has had impressive results with some vegetables.

Reflector screens, A-frames and trellises are some of the inventions these weatherwise gardeners have come up with. You may not be able to adapt all of them to your area, but they may spark an idea of how you can make the most out of the climate you live with.

Soil thermometer and maximum-minimum thermometer were used to measure effect of various plastic mulches and coverings.

A sheet of corrugated Filon arched over a row of plastic mulched peppers to increase the nighttime temperatures.

Mulches of various kinds modify the soil temperatures, save on water, and deter weeds so that the gardener can spend more time relaxing in the garden as witnessed in this picture.

Plastic mulches, either black or clear, modify the plants' growing environment.

Shade cloth and other materials can be used to protect tender trees and plants from adverse effects of the wind and sun.

# Mulches as modifiers

Mulching is one of gardening's oldest techniques. The English word was probably derived from the German vernacular *molsch,* meaning soft and rotten. It is probable then, that the ancient mulch must have been a litter of straw that gardeners found kept the soil cool and moist. From the very beginning gardeners have used mulches as a means of modifying the growing environment of plants.

Dr. J. W. Courter, an Extension Specialist in Small Fruit and Vegetable Crops at the University of Illinois, and secretary of the National Association of Plastics in Agriculture, describes a mulch as, "any substance such as straw, sawdust, plastic or paper spread on the ground to protect the roots of plants from heat, cold or drought, or to keep fruit clean. Specifically, mulch modifies the soil and air microclimate in which a plant is growing."

A mulch, then, can be either organic or a manufactured material such as polyethylene film (plastic) aluminum foil or paper.

## The effect of the sun

When the sun's rays reach the earth they are absorbed or reflected back depending on what kind of surface they hit. The rays that warm the objects they hit are "short" rays. The object heated reradiates the stored heat, but with a different wave length: the long rays.

The short rays of the sun travel through glass, translucent paper, clear plastic film, and containers of all kinds.

The nature of the soil cover you add as a mulch determines the input of the heat stored. The clear plastic mulch allows the short rays of the sun to enter the soil, but traps loss of heat, increasing soil temperatures by 10 degrees or more. A thick layer of organic matter such as sawdust or similar material reduces the input of heat. A cover of a reflective material such as aluminum foil or white coated plastic will reflect the short rays of the sun and drop the soil temperature below that of soil which is directly exposed to the sun's rays.

Polyethylene film has been used as a mulch by commercial farmers and university researchers for over 10 years, but for the home gardener it's something of a new concept, and may take some getting use to.

## Experiment station report

The following letter from J. W. Courter gives a comparative picture of the use of plastics in the home garden. The letter reads:

"Plastics can be of great benefit to home gardeners to modify (hopefully improve it!) the environment in which plants are growing. This is accomplished by modifying soil temperature, conserving soil moisture, controlling weeds, preventing root injury due to close cultivation or hoeing, maintaining good soil structure by preventing crusting and compaction of the soil, reflection of light to repel insects, modify air temperatures for optimum growth, improve soil moisture holding capacity and provide economical means of water distribution (trickle irrigation). Then of course, plastics find many other uses as pots, flats, labels, bird control netting, etc.

"One of the real problems is educating the gardener on how a

particular plastic acts (modifies) on the environment, which vegetable or crop plant will be benefited by that change, and how to use the material in question.

"Ordinary polyethylene film, available in rolls three or four feet wide and 1 to 1.5 mils thickness, makes an excellent mulch. It is true that clear film will warm the soil more than black film. Black film, however, prevents weeds from growing underneath because it excludes light needed for their growth. Therefore, we promote the use of black film rather than clear film for home gardens. The exception would be where we would want to promote early development of sweet corn or some other early seeded crop. We may or may not want to leave the film in place for the entire season depending on whether or not a chemical herbicide is used. This is a limitation for the home gardener.

"The use of clear polyethylene film also can be used to promote germination of early vegetables. I have seen it used very successfully for covering lettuce, radishes, and even early potatoes. The film is removed after the seedlings emerge from the soil. In the case of potatoes, slits may be cut to allow the plants to grow through the film. The home gardener may then leave the film in place and cover it with an organic mulch such as straw or even sawdust. Or the home gardener can make his own slit mulch for corn, beans, etc. So you can see that both clear and black may be used as long as the gardener understands the advantages and drawbacks of each.

"After the crop plant gains size and shades the mulch, the mulch has *less effect* on soil temperature. The warming or cooling effect of the mulch, I feel, has its greatest influence early in plant development.

*A test being conducted on the effects of black plastic mulch on corn plantings at a Cooperative Extension station.*

*Extension agent, Duane Hatch, shown here in demonstration garden, proves clear plastic mulch will add extra warmth needed to ripen melon crops in western Oregon's cool summers. Garden is shown here with the clear plastic mulched beds ready for planting.*

# How to install plastic mulches

These photos (a collection from various university experiment stations) show a step-by-step procedure in a typical installation of black plastic mulch.

1. *A shallow furrow or trench is dug on each side of the row the approximate width of the plastic.*

2. *Secure end of plastic at end of row.*

3. *The plastic is rolled out evenly along the row. Edges of plastic are secured by burying them in a trench and covering with soil.*

4. *A "bulb-planter" is an excellent tool to cut plastic and dig small hole for transplant. Edges of the tool should be sharpened with a file. Cutting a cross-shaped slit in the plastic and manually digging a small hole is an effective alternate, but not as fast. Size of slit will depend on the size of root ball you intend to plant.*

5. *Here a finished planting hole awaits a transplant in a Jiffy 7 pellet. In hard soil a small amount of soil substitute can be used in hole to give transplants root system a good start.*

6. *Transplant as usual.*

7. *The look of the planted row. Watering the trench on either side of the row works. Side seepage irrigates the row.*

8. *Properly done the results should look like this.*

Black plastic mulch has received a real workout in experimental stations as shown here at the Dixon Springs Agriculture Center, University of Illinois at Simpson.

A new degradable paper mulch from Gulf States Paper in black and brown.

An experimental planting of many varieties of vegetables using a black plastic mulch.

A bumper crop of bush habit pumpkins of the Cinderella variety growing on black plastic mulch. The plastic mulch helps to reduce the rotting of many vegetables.

Later other factors such as uniform soil moisture, good aeration and less compaction of the soil, and possibly greater availability of nutrients become more important. Increased soil temperature is not enough to explain yield increases. In fact when all natural environmental conditions are near ideal some vegetables may not show response to mulch. In some years deep-rooted vegetables such as tomatoes may show little benefit from mulching. In contrast shallow-rooted vegetables such as vine crops (cucumbers, etc.) show a response in most years. Use of mulches certainly can be justified for reasons other than yield increases.''

**Black plastic film.** Black polyethylene has built itself a solid reputation for increasing yields and speeding up ripening of melons, eggplant, peppers and summer squash. In areas where early season temperatures are less than ideal for these warm weather crops, yields of muskmelon in experimental plots have been increased up to 4 times over that of non-mulched plants.

The increase in soil temperature is given credit for the remarkable speed-up of growth. However, temperature readings show that the increase is generally in the 3° to 6° range, sometimes only 2°.

The temperature of the film soars high on a warm sunny day and kicks back a great deal of heat to the air above it, rather than transferring it to the soil. Insulating air pockets, between the film and the soil surface, retard heat transfer from the black film to the soil.

Make sure that the soil is damp when the mulch is applied so that there is sufficient moisture under the mulch for the mulch to retain. Dry soil should not be mulched unless there is ample water available to soak the beds after mulching.

Subsequent watering through plastic mulches is not a problem and the advent of drip irrigation systems will make watering under mulches a water-saving operation. See pages 22-23 about drip irrigation. Users of plastic mulches now take care of water needs by cutting upside-down T-slits in the plastic when watering with sprinklers, or running water through the planting holes, or laying a soaker hose under the plastic or by penetration from the side of the mulched rows.

### Demonstration garden report

Duane Hatch, Extension Agent in Eugene, Oregon brings some of the Oregon State University's research findings to the gardening public through the "Hatch Patch" demonstration garden. One proof-of-the-pudding has been his experience with plastic mulches. He reports:

"A layer of plastic over the soil aids greatly with warm season crops such as tomatoes, melons, peppers and squash. The warming of the soil will promote 10 to 14 days earlier maturity and higher yields with tomatoes. Melons, seeded about the 10th of June gave us ripe cantaloupe and watermelon by mid-September.

"We demonstrated that clear plastic is better than black plastic because the sun's energy is expanded on the soil rather than on the top part of the plastic. The weeds were not a major problem under the clear plastic if temperatures of 90° or more occurred to burn off the weeds. In 1974 we aren't getting enough heat to burn off the weeds, and we have had to lift the plastic and do some hand weeding.

"The hills of squash and melons were planted through an X cut in the plastic. With the amount of water that goes through the planting hole and around the edge of the plastic, no special watering was necessary."

In another experimental planting in Oregon several tomato varieties were tested. We quote here from the Oregon Vegetable Digest: "In 1973, 13 tomato varieties were tested at the North Willamette Experiment Station for their adaptability to the northern Willamette Valley.

"One of the growing beds was covered with black polyethylene plastic (1½ mils thick). Three plants of each variety were set 4 feet apart in the center of the bed. For irrigation, a porous wall tube ("Viaflo" by DuPont) was placed on the bed surface near the plants. Tubing was placed beneath the plastic mulch. A hole cut in the mulch permitted plants to be set. Plants were tied to a trellis of woven wire which was installed soon after planting.

"Earliest tomatoes were from un-mulched plants, but the yield of marketable fruit from plants grown with the plastic mulch was increased by an average of 114 percent over that of unmulched plants. In addition, plastic mulch also increased fruit size an average of 13 percent, saved on irrigation and prevented weed growth."

### Plastic and the home gardener.

Not all home gardeners are willing to try plastic film for a mulch. We did receive a letter, however, which told of one home gardener's experience

with black plastic mulch that might serve as an inducement to other home gardeners.

The letter came from Gus Gagis of Wayne, New Jersey. He told us that he had difficulty finding the recommended plastic (3 feet wide, 1½ mils thick) but did come across a commercially available black plastic, 4 mils thick in a 10 x 25 foot size. He purchased two of these sheets and covered a 15 x 25 foot garden area with the plastic, "wall-to-wall," rather than just the rows as is normally recommended.

It was a little difficult for neighbors and other gardeners to accept this black, shiny surface as a vegetable garden. Gus reported, "I must admit that the sight of this 'black garden' evoked many wisecracks and skeptical comments from both family and friends alike, but I persevered." That was in the early stages; the plants grew so rapidly that the value of the black plastic soon became obvious, and the plastic itself *less* obvious. . .

In a few weeks' time, the growth of the vegetables had nearly covered the

*Tomatoes growing on black plastic mulch without support in Dixon Springs.*

*Tomatoes growing on mulch and in tall wire cages (tall cages need good support). Also, an irrigation line is under the mulch to provide water to the plant.*

plastic so that the soil temperature was doubly modified.

A dry spell started around the 9th of July and has lasted through the last report we had on July 23rd. The watering demand was not as great as it would have been in an open garden, and only required an occasional soaking by inserting a garden hose under the plastic and letting the water spread. Gus had taken advantage of previous rains with T-shaped slits in the plastic.

Since this was a first time garden for Gus Gagis there is no way to compare this year's crop with last year's with regard to earliness or increase in yield, but he said, "when I compared notes with other home gardeners who were severe critics of my experiment initially, my yield to date far surpasses all of those I have spoken to." And he seems to be the first one to carry his vegetable trophies in for those in the office. "And one thing's for sure," Gus told us, "not only my immediate family, but all my relatives really enjoy the extra bounty from the 'black garden.'

*Tomatoes growing on experimental aluminum foil coated paper mulch.*

*Commercial strawberry field in Southern California. Yes, plastic mulching is a commercial practice on a big scale in some areas of the country.*

*The basic drawback of plastic mulches is they must be removed at end of season.*

*The future promises to bring degradable plastic mulches which will deteriorate and can be incorporated into the garden soil at the end of the growing season.*

*Experimental plot at Dixon Springs Agricultural Center showing an aluminum foil mulch. The foil cools the soil, the black stripe warms the planting zone.*

*Squash plant growing on sky-blue plastic mulch that reportedly repels some insects.*

# The future and plastic mulches

Despite its many strong points, there are a few drawbacks of plastic mulches.

First, as with any mulch, there is the work involved in applying the mulch to the soil. Applying a plastic mulch requires more preliminary work than an organic mulch does. (See photographs, page 9)

Secondly, hand-planting is necessary through any of the plastic or paper mulches. If your garden area is not very large, this isn't much of a consideration, but for the commercial farmer using plastic mulches it can be very time consuming.

Finally, because plastic mulches are not degradable, they must be removed at the end of the season which can be a messy job as well as adding a disposal problem.

There is considerable research

presently taking place in the field of plastic mulches, especially in the area of developing a degradable mulch which has all the beneficial properties of plastic. One company, Gulf States Paper Corporation of Tuscaloosa, Alabama, manufactures a paper mulch with a thin coating of polyethylene in 24 and 36-inch widths in rolls of 50 to 100 feet. Two colors are offered: natural brown for summer use; black for winter. As a summer mulch it reduces water evaporation, evens out soil temperatures, stops weed growth, prevents fruit rot and increases crop yield. In addition it's a degradable product, and can be cultivated into the soil after the season is over. Like a plastic mulch, it is laid over the soil and holes are cut in the paper for transplants or seeds.

There is also a current interest in aluminum and steel foils for mulching vegetables. These materials reflect the sun's rays and effectively cool the soil. This characteristic may limit the use of reflective mulches in some

areas, but may prove advantageous for main crop production when cooler soils are desired. The reflective characteristics increase the light for plant growth and also have been reported to repel certain harmful insects.

The application of a black stripe down the center of aluminum foil mulch seems to improve the growth of warm season crops. (See photograph above)

Home gardeners should also know that a combination of plastic and organic mulches can be very effective. The same gardener who used a plastic mulch for early spring soil warm-up doesn't need to worry if summer temperatures are too hot for plastic. Just add an organic mulch over the top of the plastic to shield it from the direct rays of the sun. In the desert where summer temperatures of more than 100 degrees are the rule, black plastic for weed control, covered with an organic mulch such as bark chips, is a good growing combination for many plants and shrubs.

# Organic mulches

The plastic mulches may have great advantages in increasing crop yields and in weed control, but they in no way deny the value of organic mulch. Throughout the garden an organic mulch will benefit plant growth in many ways and at the same time give the garden a well-groomed look.

Remember that the values of organic mulches are summer-time values—reducing soil temperatures and water saving. The vegetable gardener especially should understand that.

An application of an organic mulch in early spring will slow up the natural warming of the soil as spring advances. As an insulating blanket it reduces solar radiation into the soil. As a result, frost hazards are greater with a mulched bed.

**In the vegetable garden.** If you find yourself going over the soil with a cultivator, after a rain or after watering, in order to break up the surface crust, then you need a mulch. Raindrops do a cementing job by packing the small particles between the larger ones so that the pores are plugged and neither water nor rain can enter. A mulch breaks the pressure of the water drops and pore space remains open.

**Weed control.** For weed control the organic mulch must be thick enough so that weed seedlings can't go through it on their own stored food. Perennial weeds will thrive in spite of organic mulches, or because of them. Black plastic will take care of all kinds of weeds and grasses and it can be used as a base for any of the organic mulches.

**Conserves moisture.** Mulches slow down the evaporation of water from the upper 6 to 8 inches of soil. Tests show that merely shading the bare soil will reduce evaporation as much as 30 percent, but a straw mulch will reduce evaporation as much as 70 percent.

A mulch not only saves water, but it helps maintain a more even moisture supply in the upper layers of the soil.

**The richest layers.** By insulating the top few inches of the soil from the sun's heat and maintaining soil moisture to the surface of the soil, a mulch gives the roots a free run in the richest layers of the soil. Tests show that plant roots under the mulch develop as extensive a deep root

*Here a mulch of ground bark cools the soil around a strawberry patch. Soil temperatures which reach extremes are damaging to the roots of many plants.*

*This man is applying a thick layer of straw to protect tomato plants.*

*A good crop of hay will sprout in the garden unless the straw has been sterilized.*

# The pluses & minuses of mulches

| Mulch | Change in soil temperature | Performance |
|---|---|---|
| CLEAR PLASTIC | +10 | Short rays of sun penetrate clear plastic and warm soil; plastic traps evaporating water. Increases early growth in cool season, also stimulates weed growth beneath plastic. |
| BLACK PLASTIC | +6 | Short rays heat black plastic which in turn warm soil. Solves weed problem. Increases crop yields of many crops. Protects fruit of vine crops from rot. See text. |
| BROWN PAPER MULCH | as much as −8 | Light brown paper mulch with thin plastic coating reflects most of the short rays from the sun. It's biodegradable. Soil temperatures are as much as 8° cooler than first inches of exposed soil. No weeds. |
| ALUMINUM COATED PLASTIC & FOIL | as much as −10 | Reflective surface bounces back short rays from the sun. Soil temperatures are as much as 10° cooler than top inches of exposed soil. Research findings show that reflective surfaces repel aphids. |
| ORGANIC MULCHES | as much as −10 | Thick mulch of organic matter stops sun's rays before they hit the soil. Soil surface layer as much as 10 degrees cooler than exposed soil. Stops most annual weeds if applied thick enough. Needs yearly additions. |

*A home garden in Grand Rapids, Michigan, where straw mulch is used in a combination planting of vegetables and flowers. Any organic mulch that is not too decomposed promotes granulation or the clinging together of particles of soil. When such material is decomposing, a sticky substance is secreted by soil microorganisms.*
*This secretion plays an important role in soil granulation, especially in heavy soils. When adding a mulch to improve soil structure, be sure and add enough to physically change the soil structure.*

*Here a home gardener experiments with many different forms of climate modification. Tar paper and newspaper, several layers thick, are satisfactory mulches but deteriorates quickly. Plastic jugs provide early frost protection.*

*Grass clippings must be spread in a thin and even layer to prevent rotting, and the resulting bad odor. It is best used when it has had time to dry out. Do not use grass clippings which have been treated with weed killers.*

system as they do under bare soil. The surface roots are an added bonus.

Of course, if the lower layers of the soil are unfavorable to full root development such as with heavy clay that drains slowly, the plant will concentrate most to the roots near the surface of the soil.

**In the vegetable garden,** a mulch beneath unstaked tomatoes, summer squash, and cucumbers lessens the loss of fruit through rot. A tomato sitting on damp soil invites the soil bacteria to do their normal thing. Muddy splashes of rain may start rot in lettuce.

**How thick a mulch?** Apply organic mulches 1 to 2 inches thick for the fine materials such as sawdust. Coarse or fluffy materials can be applied 3 to 4 inches thick. Materials such as straw or chopped corncobs may be covered with a more attractive mulch.

Untreated sawdust will cause some degree of nitrogen shortage. Soil bacteria go to work on the sawdust, and take their necessary supply of nitrogen from the soil. The loss is not as great as when sawdust is mixed in the soil. A good rule of thumb measurement is to increase the amount of fertilizer regularly used for the crop by ¼ when using a sawdust mulch.

**Caution in applying.** Apply mulch evenly. When using a mulch that becomes soggy when wet, don't pack it around the stem or trunk of the plant. When the mulch is thoroughly wet, pull it back a few inches from the stem or trunk so there is free air circulation to the base of the plant.

**Gradually improves soil structure.**
Mulches should be maintained at the original thickness. As the mulch thins down, add new material. As the mulch decomposes or is washed into the soil the structure of the soil is gradually improved.

The definition of waste material is changing. Less and less of the green material is burned or buried. What comes out of the soil goes back into the soil to restore and improve it. Many "waste" products are now popular nursery items—sawdust, bark in all sizes, manure and more. But if you look around you may discover a waste product of agriculture that is peculiar to your area. And local agricultural by-products are usually less expensive than packaged and processed ones. Where grapes are pressed there is pomace. Where nuts are shelled there are shells which can be ground or pulverized. Where there's a cider mill there's apple pomace.

**Buckwheat hulls.** This material is fine-textured, and may blow around if used in windy places. It is long-lived and has a good neutral color, making it quite satisfactory in landscape plantings. There may be some odor during hot, humid weather.

**Chunk bark.** Redwood and fir are the most popular forms available. This material is long-lasting, and is available in various sizes to fit many landscape needs.

**Compost.** An excellent mulch and soil conditioner that you make at home by composting various kinds of non-woody plant refuse, such as grass clippings, leaves, plant tops from the vegetable and flower garden, etc. The partially decomposed material rates as one of the best organic mulches, although it may not be the most attractive. Many gardening books provide instructions on how to make compost.

**Corncobs (crushed).** Another excellent and usually inexpensive mulch. May be colored for special uses in landscape plantings, or weathered if the light color of the fresh material bothers you. Additional nitrogen should be applied.

**Corncobs (whole).** Used to a limited extent in greenhouse beds and commercial vegetable plantings. Also satisfactory in utility gardens where appearance isn't a major consideration.

**Hay (leguminous).** Used mostly in farm gardens, since the material is more likely to be available. No additional nitrogen is required.

**Hops (spent).** Can sometimes be obtained from local breweries. Has an excellent color and is noninflammable. The odor may be offensive but usually subsides in a few weeks.

**Lawn clippings.** This material is best used when dry. If applied fresh, it should be spread loosely; otherwise, it mats down, produces heat during decomposition, and gives off an offensive odor. Do not use grass clippings if the lawn has been treated with a weed-killer such as 2,4-D or related compounds.

**Leafmold.** Obtained by composting leaves in the fall of the year. If properly handled, the material should be partially decomposed by spring. A good mulch, but hard to apply evenly and not particularly attractive.

**Leaves.** Used rather extensively in areas where trees are abundant. The least expensive mulch available,

*One gardener reports: One year I was sold on trying straw as a mulch. The trouble was that the straw was oat straw and I managed to get a beautiful crop of oats wherever the straw was used over the soil—but not where the black plastic was laid down.*

*Blueberries grow well in an organic mulch such as sawdust. Weathered or partially decomposed sawdust is preferred over fresh material because of the danger of heat build-up which could injure tender young plant roots. Sod plantings between rows give convenience in walking and plant care.*

but better if composted. Nitrogen additions will probably be needed.

**Manure (strawy).** Makes an excellent mulch in utility or farm gardens if partially decomposed. But be sure that it hasn't been treated with odor-reducing chemicals. These substances are sometimes injurious to growing plants. No additional nitrogen applications are needed with this mulch.

**Mushroom compost (spent).** This material is often available in areas where commercial mushrooms are produced. It is usually inexpensive, and has a good color that blends into the landscape.

**Peanut hulls.** Can be obtained in some local garden centers, especially in areas where peanuts are processed. This is an excellent mulch, and is usually quite attractive.

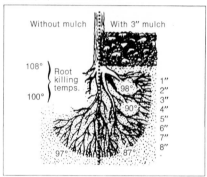

**Peat moss.** This is one of the most commonly used mulches. It is quite rich-looking when used properly, but the cost of the material is often prohibitive when large areas are to be covered. Various particle sizes are available on the market. The fine grade has a tendency to blow away. When very dry, peat sheds water rather than allowing it to soak in.

**Pecan shells.** A good long-lasting mulch with pleasing color and texture. Homeowners who have used it regularly report some problems with birds and rodents.

**Pine needles.** This material makes a light, airy, attractive mulch. Since pine needles are moderately acid, they are especially desirable for acid-loving plants such as azaleas, blueberries, etc.

**Poultry litter.** In many areas, this material is available from poultry farms. The litter material may be straw, sawdust, crushed corn-cobs, wood chips, etc. The poultry manure mixed with it takes care of the nitrogen requirement. Apply this mulch sparingly until you know how much to use without damaging plants from an overdose of fertilizer.

◁ *Bark used as mulch in mixed flower garden.*

**Sawdust.** A very common mulch material in areas where readily available. A nitrogen deficiency is almost inevitable unless fertilizer is applied regularly. Reports of toxic materials in the sawdust have not been substantiated by experiment station research.

**Shredded hardwood bark.** In recent years, this material has become a popular item in garden stores. It makes an excellent mulch that is easy to apply and very attractive in landscape settings. Shredded bark usually lasts longer than peat moss, adds valuable organic matter to the soil.

**Straw.** Used for winter protection and sometimes as a summer mulch. It is unsightly and also highly inflammable. Should not be used where a cigarette could be carelessly flipped into it.

**Wood chips or wood shavings.** This material has become available in large quantities in recent years, since it can no longer be burned as a waste product by the mills. Wood chips decompose slowly, but may be the cause of nitrogen deficiency if additional fertilizer is not applied.

## What to expect from organic mulches

Since organic mulches are derived from plant material, decomposition does occur, and several important effects to the soil and to plant growth will be apparent to gardeners.

**Physical effects.** Mulches dilute the soil and usually increase root growth. The addition of such mulches as crushed corncobs, sphagnum peat moss, or shredded bark to the soil brings an almost immediate effect. Aeration is improved in clay soils, and the water-holding capacity is increased in sandy soils.

If not too decomposed, the mulch will promote granulation or the clinging together of soil particles. During decomposition of organic material, soil microorganisms secrete a sticky substance that plays an important role in soil granulation. This process is particularly important in heavy soil types.

Because of the mulch layer, the soil structure (arrangement of particles) is not disturbed by pelting rains. Cultivating the soil when it is too wet destroys good soil structure. When mulches are used, no cultivation is necessary.

*"Using mulches in the home landscape"*
*by Marvin C. Carbonneau*
*Dept. of Horticulture, Univ. of Illinois*

*This mulch of bark chips not only benefits the roses by cooling the soil but also improves the soil structure as it gradually breaks down; should be replaced yearly.*

*The attractive color and texture of this ground pecan shell mulch makes it a decorative part of the landscape design as well as weed control.*

# The determined gardener

There is a certain breed of home gardeners—an adventurous bunch determined to harvest a crop, despite the odds of the weather or the first and last frost dates. They don't always succeed in harvesting their late crops of tomatoes or corn or whatever, but the ideas and methods that the determined gardener comes up with should interest any fellow gardener.

The creed of the determined gardener is to find a way to "cheat the season," either by lengthening it, making it warmer or cooler, wetter or drier, or by providing protection from the wind.

A prime example of the ingenuity of such gardeners is seen in the photographs on the left. Intent upon growing corn in a very shaded back yard, this gardener came up with reflective panels to increase the amount of sunlight and direct it into the only available ground space he had. Tall hedges flanked both sides of the corn patch which effectively blocked both the morning and afternoon sun. In the first experiment in 1973 aluminum foil was stapled to plastic and hung on both the east and west sides of the planting area. The corn crop was perfect except in those rows next to the hedge. The next year reflective metalized plastic was glued to plywood panels and hinged to a wooden frame. The metalized plastic and the adjustable angle of reflection proved to be more efficient. The gardener reported that it was, "the best corn I'd ever tasted!"

Many of the methods gardeners use to "cheat the season" are not new at all. For years gardeners in Europe have made the most out of a small amount of sun by training fruit trees against a wall, preferably a light colored one. The reflected light and increased heat next to the wall provide enough warmth and light to ripen fruit that would not mature if grown out in the open.

Originally the word *espalier* was defined as a trellis upon which a plant is trained. Now the expression *to espalier* is used loosely to mean *to train* plants to grow flat against a wall trellis, fence or free-standing panel. The training may take a formal pattern such as repeated horizontals or the plant may be allowed to develop in a natural, informal pattern.

By training fruit trees against the wall in this manner, you not only make the most out of the sun, but you can

*The problem: In the only space available for a planting of corn an 8 foot hedge stopped the morning sun; a 10 foot hedge put the garden in shade in late afternoon. In the first experiment aluminum foil was stapled to plastic and hung on both east and west sides of planted area. Corn crop was perfect except in rows next to hedge. The next year reflective panels of metalized plastic with adjustable angle of reflection were more efficient.*

*Reflective walls or sheets can be utilized to intensify solar energy and produce food in an otherwise shady spot.*

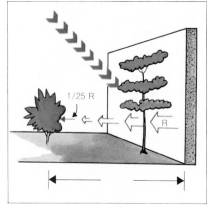

1/25 R

*Espalier training to a warm, light wall can produce fruit where a free-standing tree would be barren.*

conserve space. The small space gardener may or may not be interested in espaliering. They do, however, get the idea as a space saving method. The idea that you can enjoy 3 or 4 varieties of dwarf apples on a 15 foot long trellis makes good space saving sense. And many commercial fruit growers are now finding out that they get a higher production of many fruits by crowding dwarf and semi-dwarf trees together in hedge rows.

Many gardeners are successful with standard trees for this type gardening. However, the dwarf varieties are more adaptable to trellis training. Check your local nurseries for recommended dwarf varieties.

*Wooden frames, wire or netting are used in traditional flat wall type or on A-frame trellis. They conserve space, produce better fruit and make harvest easier.*

*Trellis training is an easy way to expand growing season by placing plants in a section of the garden where there is more light and heat.*

*Almost any vining vegetable will adapt to trellis growing. The A-frame allows flexibility in placement to receive fullest benefits of the sun.*

*Cucumbers grow straighter when allowed to hang freely from a trellis.*

19

# The A-frame

The A-frame is an extension of the trellis idea, except that it was designed with vining vegetables in mind. Vegetables that were once considered as space wasters in the small garden are now taken skyward. The small fruited watermelon, winter squash, melons and just about anything that vines can be trained vertically. We have found that the A-frame type of trellis has several advantages over the vertical trellis:

✔ The A-frame can be positioned to take advantage of maximum sunlight and heat on one side, leaving the opposite for growing crops which demand a cooler environment. In watching the growth of pole beans on trellises and cucumbers on A-frames, we noticed that we got a better crop of vegetables if the position of the trellis ran east and west. Perhaps it really doesn't make any difference, but the north side of

the trellis was well suited for growing lettuce during the summer months.

✔ The frame can be converted into a tent for early spring frost protection. If you try making a row tent out of an A-frame by covering it with plastic, realize that the amount of ventilation needed with plastic covers is always a problem to the gardener. Learn what will work for you by daring to experiment.

✔ Such vegetables as pole beans and cucumbers are easy to see when the ''trellis'' is on a 45 to 70 degree slant. There's less chance of hiding in the leaves. And cucumbers grow straighter when hanging down.

✔ The frame may be latticed on one side and open on the other. This variation makes for easy harvesting of vegetables that hang down.

✔ The A-frame supports itself. No heavy permanent posts are needed.

✔ It can be hinged to fold flat for storage.

*Hotkaps allow the sun's rays to penetrate during the day which sometimes causes problems with excessive heat build-up. Remove during the day if warm weather is expected and replace at night. Small hole permits ventilation.*

*Wire mesh gives protection from birds and animals. Can be covered with plastic . . .*

*to serve as row greenhouses which warm the soil and stop damage from winds.*

*Gallon size bottomless plastic jugs are useful protectors for tender plants.*

*Above: A small hinged A-frame increases spring soil temperatures. Open ends allow circulation. It can be easily picked up and stored when not needed.*

*Right: A 4 x 8 foot clear fiberglass panel is arched over part of a row at sunset each day, removed next morning. Soil and air temperatures read at 11 p.m., were higher than those in the open row. Plastic covered peppers grew faster, larger than those in open ground.*

# Plastic-the pluses and minuses

Before using any kind of plastic in the garden for frost protection, be it plastic jugs or plastic draped over an A-frame, there are a few things the gardener should know.

*Where* you use such early-season growing aids as row covers and plastic jugs is all important. In areas where temperatures are consistently cool such aids fulfill their function very well. But if you live in an area where a stretch of cool spring weather may be broken by temperatures equal to a hot summer day, the gardener may find a plastic-covered plant cooked to death.

Good ventilation is the key to avoid disaster. A row cover, with both ends open, should provide enough ventilation to allow the excessive heat to escape. If there is no ventilation through plastic covers of any kind, the gardener should remove them on a warm day and replace them again at night.

In one of our test gardens we found a way to keep plastic row covers warm at night. We put large plastic bleach bottles full of water inside the row cover. During the day the sun warms the water; at night it slowly gives off heat and keeps the plants inside the cover several degrees warmer than the outside air.

One of our gardeners who disliked the traditional hotkaps reports: "We have had good luck with respect to late, light frosts with 2-pound coffee cans, both the top and the bottom removed. We put them over our tomatoes, eggplants, and peppers and leave them for a couple of weeks. Occasionally the tips of the leaves get burnt by the hot metal on contact, but the damage is not permanent. The advantage of the open-ended can is that you don't have to lift it every morning and then replace every night. Of course, it's not protection against heavy frost, but one would not normally be putting out tender plants that early.

One of our gardeners in California stretches the tomato season with the aid of plastic:

We extend our tomato season by as much as three weeks by laying a wide strip of black plastic over each row at night. This year we will do the same with peppers and eggplants.

Having frosts September 20-30 we lose a lot of fruit unless we protect it this way.

*When protecting tender plants from frost, remove the protective covering during the day to allow the sun's rays to heat the soil. Cover at night to trap the long rays.*

*Shingles (top) protect young plants. Wooden crate gives protection to melon when temperatures are high.*

*Above: Shade cloth on a wooden box protects young tree from sun and wind. Below: Wire mesh keeps away animals. Bottom portion of trunk is painted white as a protection from the sun.*

*Various materials such as cardboard can be used to protect young tree trunks from attacking pests and sun damage.*

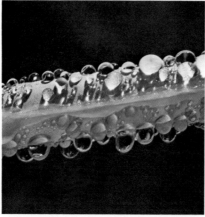

*A close-up shot of a section of viaflow tubing. Water passes through micron-sized openings in the hose walls.*

*Here a viaflow system is being laid down and will be covered with black plastic mulch at a university test station. Viaflow operates on low water pressure.*

*Viaflow under clear plastic mulched strawberries. Commercial farmers and home gardeners benefit from these systems.*

*Viaflow soaker-oozer irrigation system in a home garden placed next to young pepper plants. Viaflow can be buried in the ground or placed on top as it is here.*

*Drip emitter supplies a new planting of squash with water. Drip irrigation methods can make a little water go a long way in the home garden.*

*Multiple lines of viaflow can be run off of one hose. Several manufacturers of drip/trickle irrigation systems now make products for the home gardener.*

# Drip/trickle irrigation

Especially in areas with limited water supplies, the idea of making a little water go a long way is nothing new. But today home gardeners are hearing some new words about irrigation techniques and equipment—such as emitters, spot-spitters, Dew-Hose, Jumbo-oozers, Viaflow, Twin-wall, Drip-Eze are a few. After years of testing in thousands of acres of orchards, row crops, nursery operations, the drip/trickle system of irrigation is being offered to the home gardener. The systems offered are not fool proof. Manufacturers are changing parts in the systems as more tests are made. But the potential advantages of drip irrigation in shrub and tree plantings, home orchards, vineyards and vegetable gardens are so great that the home garden experiment seems worthwhile.

The advantages of drip irrigation are noted in the following quotes from Dr. Falih Aljibury, Irrigation and Water Technologist from the University of California.

"While generally considered as a new irrigation method, the basic concept of drip irrigation has been practiced since the beginning of this century by nurseries growing fruit trees and ornamental plants. However, it has only been in the past few years that this concept has been expanded to include application in many crops grown in the field as well as under nursery and greenhouse conditions.

"With drip irrigation, the water drops onto the soil surface without disturbing the soil structure, so that the water can seep between soil particles. Once in the soil, the water moves by capillary to the surrounding areas.

"Drip irrigation drops the water onto the ground through one or more emitters located adjacent to each tree or plant.

"In drip irrigation one tries to replenish the water on an almost daily basis. This amount of water being equal to the water used by the plant or tree since the last irrigation. In other words, drip irrigation does not store water for a long future tree use, but rather constantly replaces water that has already been used.

On the following page we chart the workings of a composite automatic drip system as it is put together for various commercial uses. Home garden units are modifications of this system.

# Composite of drip irrigation systems

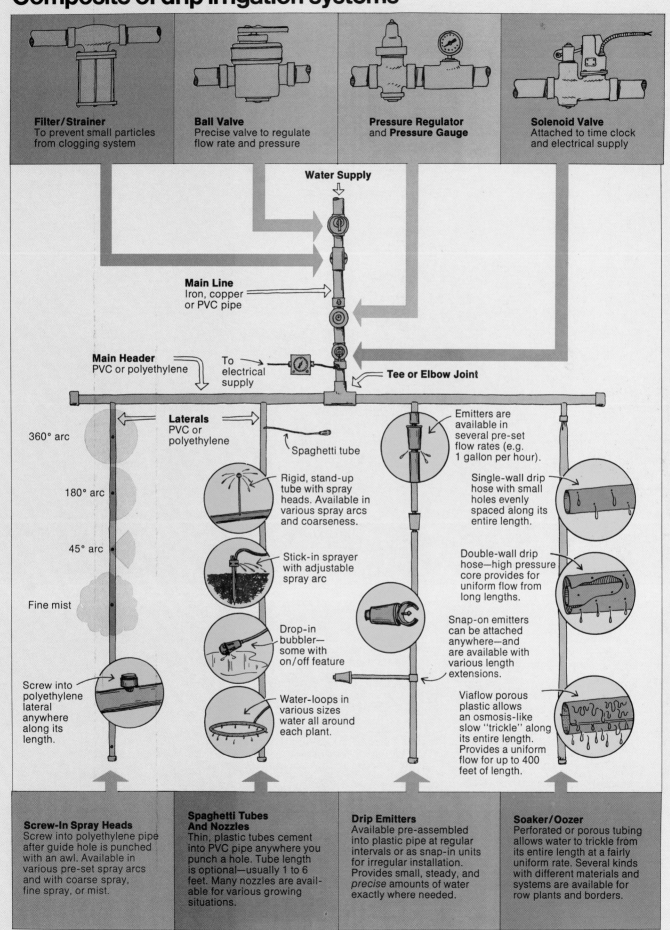

**Filter/Strainer**
To prevent small particles from clogging system

**Ball Valve**
Precise valve to regulate flow rate and pressure

**Pressure Regulator** and **Pressure Gauge**

**Solenoid Valve**
Attached to time clock and electrical supply

**Water Supply**

**Main Line**
Iron, copper or PVC pipe

**Main Header**
PVC or polyethylene

To electrical supply

**Tee or Elbow Joint**

**Laterals**
PVC or polyethylene

Spaghetti tube

360° arc

180° arc

45° arc

Fine mist

Screw into polyethylene lateral anywhere along its length.

Rigid, stand-up tube with spray heads. Available in various spray arcs and coarseness.

Stick-in sprayer with adjustable spray arc

Drop-in bubbler—some with on/off feature

Water-loops in various sizes water all around each plant.

Emitters are available in several pre-set flow rates (e.g. 1 gallon per hour).

Single-wall drip hose with small holes evenly spaced along its entire length.

Double-wall drip hose—high pressure core provides for uniform flow from long lengths.

Snap-on emitters can be attached anywhere—and are available with various length extensions.

Viaflow porous plastic allows an osmosis-like slow "trickle" along its entire length. Provides a uniform flow for up to 400 feet of length.

**Screw-In Spray Heads**
Screw into polyethylene pipe after guide hole is punched with an awl. Available in various pre-set spray arcs and with coarse spray, fine spray, or mist.

**Spaghetti Tubes And Nozzles**
Thin, plastic tubes cement into PVC pipe anywhere you punch a hole. Tube length is optional—usually 1 to 6 feet. Many nozzles are available for various growing situations.

**Drip Emitters**
Available pre-assembled into plastic pipe at regular intervals or as snap-in units for irregular installation. Provides small, steady, and *precise* amounts of water exactly where needed.

**Soaker/Oozer**
Perforated or porous tubing allows water to trickle from its entire length at a fairly uniform rate. Several kinds with different materials and systems are available for row plants and borders.

# The many advantages of raised beds

Gardeners who have been denied the luxury of a rich loamy soil have come up with a number of ways to combat the problem, and in doing so have found themselves with other advantages besides "good soil."

Many a gardener finds himself working with soil that won't support a vegetable garden. The soil may have a shallow layer of rocks or hardpan, or heavy clay that drains slowly, or some other combination that is unfriendly to plants and hard to manage.

In such problem situations, growing plants above the soil is the best answer. The soil raised above ground level is held in place by 1" or 2" boards or with railroad ties as seen in some of the pictures to the right.

One of the primary advantages of the raised bed is that the gardener has a choice when deciding what kind of soil he wants to garden in. When the bed is filled with a light-weight soil mix rich in organic matter the gardener has a very efficient vegetable growing factory.

If the mixture is light-weight, drainage through the soil is good and with soil raised above ground level, drainage away from the bed is possible. Unless the soil around the bed is flooded, the soil and the raised bed will never be waterlogged. This is seen by many gardeners as a big advantage because in a wet, cool spring the soil in the raised bed will warm up and be ready to plant weeks before regular garden soil can be seeded or worked.

If the raised bed is accessible from both sides, a width of 6 to 8' is practical. Planting, weeding and harvesting can be handled without walking in the bed. If the raised bed is alongside a fence or for any reason accessible from only one side, make the width 3 to 4'. The height of the bed should be at least 12" above the soil. If the raised bed is built 16" high and capped with 2 x 6" boards, you can sit while you weed.

A well built raised bed can support a lot of extras. Side boards can be used to hold wire frames to keep out birds and cats, or plastic covers to increase warmth or protect from the frost. Plastic covers can be used to prolong the growth of lettuce and other salad makings well into the winter.

There is another advantage to the raised bed that is seldom pointed out.

*Top: Raised beds were built in this garden to combat the heavy clay soil typical of the area. Tomatoes are grown in wire cages. Bottom: In the early spring soil warms up faster in raised beds allowing earlier planting.*

*Lettuce thrives in raised planters filled with a special light-weight soil mix.*

*An attractive multi-level raised bed garden with paths paved with white bricks.*

As a clean and neat structure, the gardener feels an obligation to keep the planting clean and neat. Weeds are more distracting in a raised bed than in an equal amount of planting space in a hidden corner of the garden.

We have talked with many gardeners who heartily endorse the use of raised beds. Instead of battling with the poor soil found in many yards, and the even poorer results from their vegetable growing attempts, the raised bed offers disillusioned gardeners an almost "instant" solution. Not only are results from growing common vegetables improved, but gardeners who garden in raised beds can be more adventurous in what they plant. If you've shied away from growing lettuce because your soil is too heavy, or didn't want to try growing carrots because your soil was too rocky, raised beds are the answer.

A gardener with limited space can afford to take measures that increase production and remove some of the hazards of conventional vegetable gardening. Inventive gardeners are rediscovering the advantages of the old frame gardens, the raised bed, the cold frame, and the hot bed. (See pages 65-67.)

Call it what you want to, it illustrates one way to concentrate the growing of vegetables in an environment free from any of the hazards in open-space gardening. The use of such a structure as a raised bed will add weeks to the growing season, early and late. The hazards of heavy rains and blistering sun during a heat wave can be averted by a choice of frames and covers. Use plastic covers when it rains, lath or shade cloth when the summer sun is blazing hot. Wire coverings have their place when wind damage is critical.

Remember that the raised bed has these points in its favor:

✔ **Speeds up spring planting.** In a wet, cool spring the soil in the raised bed will warm up and be ready for planting weeks before regular garden soils can be planted.

✔ **Can be easily modified.** Raised beds can be converted into cold frames, shaded areas, or provide protection from the wind and small animals.

✔ **Easier on the back.** You sit on the edge of the raised beds when weeding. Cultivating can be done with a putty knife instead of a hoe.

✔ **Good for the specialist.** Herb gardeners, collectors of miniatures in bulbs, cactus and succulents or whatever, appreciate the restraint and the close-to-the-eye of the raised bed.

*Railroad ties hold soil in place in a large family garden. Celery, onions and leeks are planted close together to get maximum use of space and provide a large harvest.*

*Here a raised border next to a fence gets maximum use. Tomatoes and dwarf marigolds find enough space to provide an extra harvest and a bit of color. Sunflowers add privacy.*

*When filled with a light soil, raised beds are perfect for growing any of the root crops.*

*Railroad ties frame a handsome raised bed of parsley and cabbage.*

# Climate and landscape... They work together

With a little thoughtful planning and planting, landscaping can improve both the outdoor and indoor climate of your house and yard. In this chapter we explore the principles and the applications of landscaping for a more liveable environment.

If you've ever planted a small tree from a one gallon can and wondered if it was ever going to amount to anything—the pictures on the next four pages should give you heart. The photographs record a 13-year history of the landscaping of one yard in Middlesex, New Jersey.

The house and yard belong to Raymond P. Korbobo, a landscape specialist with the Rutgers State University Extension Service. When the Korbobos first moved into the house in 1950, they decided to remove 5 large hickory trees that had shaded the rear of the house; the trees had become so large that they were undesirable, and hampered a good usage of space in the back yard.

Right after the trees were removed, the Korbobos noticed a sharp increase in temperatures inside the house during the summer months. The actions that Korbobo took, which modified both the inside and outside climates, are shown here step by step in these photographs; the captions are in his own words.

One statement of Korbobo's was particularly reassuring, "Looking ahead 13 years is an eternity— looking back—just a few moments!" With proper planting and a little tender, loving care, a plant works for you 24 hours a day, 365 days a year.

◁

*A sneak preview of the end results of 13 years of weatherwise gardening.*

**(1)** Rear of our house as we bought it in 1950. We removed 5 undesirable large shade trees and this exposed us to the full sun from the South.

**(2)** The first steps toward "instant" shade. This meant that within 3 years after the arbor (put up in 1956) we had as much shade as we would have had from trees which would have taken 10 to 15 years to grow up to the needed height. Hence— "instant" shade in three years.

**(3)** Old garage in background. New brick terrace started. Note—flooded with hot sun.

**(4)** This is early into its third year. At end of the summer the shade on the wall of the

lower floor of our house was almost 100% shaded. Note how the house (left) and summer house-garage (right) form a 90° angle. This helped trap the heat for early spring and late fall use. The fact that the large Pi Oak kept us from connecting the two structures worked to a weather advantage too—this "venturi" tube or valve speeds the air movement from a large area through a smaller opening and creates a synthetic MPH figure for the breeze! The young tree in the foreground is a very key plant in this total scheme. It was strategically placed so its afternoon shade would cool the brick terrace in mid-summer and keep the sinking sun's rays out of our eyes as we sat on the

porch. I readily admit that in my own mind I figured at least 20 years for this effect.) It took only 11 years for that tree to do its job. (*Sophora Japonica*—Chinese Scholartree). You'll see it in later shots.

**(5)** This view is from off of our property looking back to the summer house-garage. The arbor is on the left. This photograph was taken in early spring (April) and note the warmth of the entire area; we get a great deal of use out of this area early in the season.

**(6)** View from inside the summer house-garage just opposite of photograph to the above right. (White spots in bricks just happens to be chlordane granules on top of ant hills.)

**(7)** Early in the morning, October, 1960. The shade is from the large oak trees to the right and rear of the summer house.

5

6

At mid-day it will be all sun. White chrysanthemums specially planted for a garden party we held that year. Chestnut flowers!

**(8)** May 1961. Looking from far end of arbor back toward our driveway. This followed a brief spring shower—no sun—but you can tell by the shady "feeling" that it is already controlling our microclimate to our advantage. Wisteria on the arbor. Also some clematis and grape vines!

**(9)** Late April—1963. Early A.M. again. Look closely on right side of picture. The rapidly growing *Sophora Japonica* (slide #4) is already starting to spread over to

the brick terrace. We are looking due East.

**(10)** Mid-May—1963. Magnolia Kalus on right. This also blocked out the very low sun rays at day's end.

**(11)** Late March-early May—1967. Note: sun is warming the house at this cold season yet. See how big the *Sophora Japonica* is already! Compare hedges— left and right foreground—to slide #4. Hedges hide the vegetables and cut flower area to left and our daughter's duck pens on the right. Aluminum siding has been added to the house. On a sunny day such as this we could already "sit out" in comfort on the brick terrace.

7

8

9

11

10

12

13

14

(12) Mid-May—1969. There she is in all her glory—13 years later. (Looking ahead, 13 years is an eternity—looking back—just a few moments!)

(13) Mid-May—1969. A shot from our bedroom window. Looks out to the informal private area. Sophora tree now shading the bricks.

(14) May, 1969. Not only "climate control" but beautiful too!

(15) As the years have gone by we find ourselves spending more time at home, making the prolonged use of the terrace in spring and fall more important to us.

(16) Proof positive—bricks are warmer, grass is cooler. Snow on grass and bricks in my own garden.

15

16

# Altering your climate

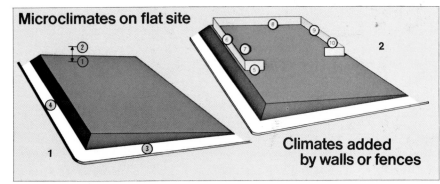

**Microclimates on flat site**

**Climates added by walls or fences**

Eventually the climate becomes your own personal concern. You live with it as it is, or you modify it within reasonable bounds to make its conditions more comfortable for you and your family activities, and for more satisfactory and productive gardening.

Most United States weather runs to extremes, from sub-zero to steaming tropical and every degree in between. Summers are too hot and winters are too cold; winds can be persistent and irritating. Transitional periods can have their pleasant days, but just as often bring destructive storms.

As the season progresses from winter toward summer, the sun appears higher in the sky as a given location moves to a more perpendicular angle to its radiation. The longer solar path at the loftier elevations also adds to the daylight hours.

Summer is hotter than winter because the higher sun angle concentrates the solar energy, and longer days give the surface of a location

*1. Even a vacant lot has more than one climate. Temperatures differ at its surface, and spots a few inches or feet above. South slopes absorb most radiation, north slopes the least. 2. Fences and walls further increase the climates. Solid ones can absorb and radiate heat; ventilated ones allow circulation and are better windbreaks. 3. The house establishes your most constant solar pattern. The north, almost perpetually shaded, is a location for hardy, cold-resistant plants. Tender varieties find the full sun of the south wall more suitable. East and west walls receive equal sunlight, but the latter is warmer because some of the morning sun energy is used to overcome the cold of the preceding night. 4. Ground treatment varies the micro-climates in warmer or cooler directions. Paving, gravel, soil, grass, and other covers all have different radiating and reflective properties. Secondary structures are immediate climate controls.*

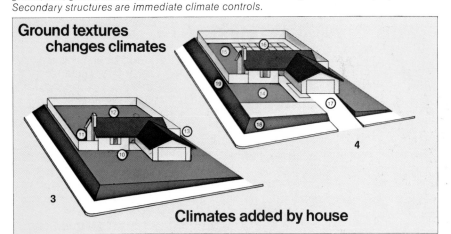

**Ground textures changes climates**

**Climates added by house**

**Landscaped for microclimates**

*1. & 2. Controlled shade zones (1. is warmer, receives afternoon sun); 3. Sun pocket—receiving noon and afternoon sun; 4. Pond—good place for shade and moisture-loving plants; 5. Morning and mid-day sun zone—wall provides some protection; 6. Full shade zone; 7. Morning sun zone; 8. Full shade zone—trees and house provide protection; 9. Partial sun zone for late afternoon radiation; 10. Variable shade zone below a tree; 11. Full sun zone; 12. Controlled shade zone provided by lath house; 13. Greenhouse—absolute climate control; 14. Variable shade zone below a tree; and 15. Full sun zone for vegetables and other sun-loving plants.*

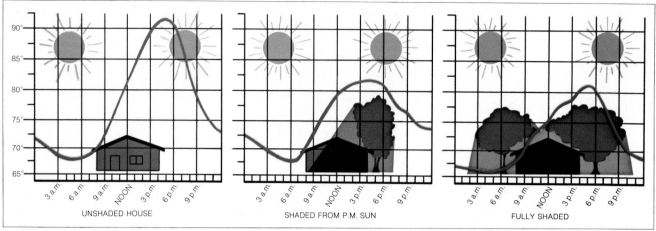

| | | |
|---|---|---|
| UNSHADED HOUSE | SHADED FROM P.M. SUN | FULLY SHADED |

*Outdoor landscaping greatly affects temperature, as well as available light, inside the house. This fact is illustrated by the above graphic profile showing temperature range inside similar homes with various density of exterior planting.*

*Like this red oak, any large shade tree creates its own climate when in foliage, adding moisture to the air. A column of warmer air goes up through the tree, causing a slight breeze at ground level by "feeding" this thermal column of ascending warm air.*

more time to accumulate the radiation. Short nights lessen the periods of heat loss.

The great orderly atmospheric movements, the persistent patterns of the high and low pressure areas, the relationship of land and water masses, and the other regulations of the macroclimates are beyond our control. Though cloud seeding by present-day rainmakers is able to alter local rainfall patterns, successful and safe weather modification on a large scale is unlikely in the predictable future.

Mesoclimates can change through the effects of human activity, however. The city, for instance, is made warmer than surrounding suburban and rural areas, as its pavement and masonry structures absorb and re-radiate more of solar energy. Irrigated cropland, dams and water storage reservoirs, and transpiration from the additional vegetation raises the humidity of formerly dry, arid valleys.

Microclimates, the little weathers

clustered about every house and yard, are the only ones over which we can exert any control through our own individual efforts. We can bend them towards our needs by thoughtful orientation of structure and plantings, by increasing or lessening radiation, and numerous other methods of exploiting their potentials.

Microclimatic modifications have limitations, of course. They can't change a general weather pattern. They can't prevent torrid conditions everywhere in a blistering midsummer desert, or provide a safe location for a sub-tropical plant in a New England winter.

They do have the capacity, though, to vary seasoned climates enough to definitely improve our living both outdoors and indoors, to get more pleasure from our recreational activities, to provide the few degrees of temperature difference which can mean survival to a tender plant on a frosty night, or to temper a dessicating wind.

*Electricity usage study: shaded houses use 2 KWH per sq. ft.; unshaded, 3.3 KWH.*

*A circular brick patio underneath a shade tree takes advantage of cool breezes created at the bases of large trees by ascending air.*

### Objectives of climatic modification

The big basic factors establishing our weather patterns—insolation, air circulation, and moisture—are the same wherever we live in the United States.

Our geographical locations determine the degrees of their intensities and the extents of their distribution. Through microclimates, we can take advantage of the big weather controls to increase or lessen the effects of prevailing conditions and modify their extremes.

Simply put, we would like to make our own particular environments either warmer or cooler, less windy or breezier, dryer or more humid. We can't make a poor climate ideal, but we can certainly improve it.

Geography differs these objectives. Along the damp, foggy northwest coast, residents invite the summer sun into their homes and gardens as much as possible. At the same time, sweltering mid-westerners need protection from it. Breezes which can circulate the sticky, humid air of the Gulf Coast and the eastern seaboard are not welcome in chillier mountain regions.

## Understanding the principles

Whatever your requirements, your best climatic controls are a good building site and weather-oriented architecture. The slope of a lot determines the amount of insolation it receives, adjacent terrain can regulate wind and other conditions. A well-designed house will provide the modifications needed for the seasons and the critical periods of the day.

But, most of us have to make do with what we have or can afford. Through thoughtful landscaping and supplementary structure, however, we can gain advantages that nature, or building contractors, neglected to give us.

### Tips for climate modification

These pointers are guides to general methods that can be explored to benefit humans and plants. In climates with wide seasonal variations, however, use controls that are useful for both summer and winter conditions. A deciduous tree, for example, gives summer shade but defoliates to allow winter sun penetration.

#### To make it warmer:

✔Maximum solar exposures.

✔Paved areas and untilled ground,

### Seasonal sun angles and day length

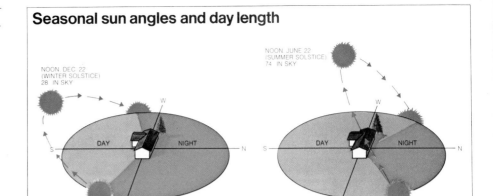

rock or masonry surfaces, south slopes for increased absorption of radiation.

✔Structural or plant "ceilings" to reflect back outgoing radiation at night.

✔Sun pockets.

✔Windbreaks and cold airflow diverters.

✔Mulches.

#### To make it cooler:

✔Shade trees and vines.

✔Overhangs, awnings, canopies (cooler in daytime, warmer at night).

✔Planted ground covers.

✔Pruning of lower growth for increased air circulation.

✔Evaporative cooling (from sprinklers and pools).

#### To make it less windy:

✔Windbreaks, baffles, diverters (planted and structural)

✔Berms.

✔Semi-enclosed outdoor living areas.

#### To make it breezier:

✔Pruning of low branches of trees.

✔Minimum low plant growth.

✔Creation of breezeways (structural and planted).

*Outdoor living areas are semi-enclosed to control wind and temperature. Shade cloth can be added over lath beams in summer.*

**To make it more humid:**

✔ Overhead planting (slows evaporation and adds transpiration).

✔ Low windbreaks.

✔ Planted ground covers.

✔ Pools, cascades, sprinklers.

**To make it dryer:**

✔ Maximum solar exposures.

✔ Maximum ventilation.

✔ Efficient drainage system.

✔ Paved ground surfaces.

Tests by agricultural stations of state universities show that what you do to the climate outside the house has a definite effect upon the climate within it. Figures quoted are from tests by Agricultural Experiment Station, Kansas State University, and Univ. of Calif. at Davis.

Shelter plantings outdoors can reduce operating expenses of heating and air conditioning units by up to one-third or more, no small consideration in times of energy shortages and rising costs.

Trees work as well through the summer, functioning as natural air conditioners to improve indoor climates and reduce energy consumption.

Properly shaded, a house has far less use for a mechanical air conditioner. If one is installed, it need operate only half as much as it would to do the same job in an unshaded structure.

Well planned landscaping can create a wealth of new comfort zones for you and your plants, and better the indoor climate of your home at the same time. Each tree and shrub changes the conditions around it. Every alteration you make will have some microclimatic effect on your property.

# Make the sun work with you, not against you

The sun is a gigantic fiery furnace 93 million miles away from us. Its tremendous energy bombards us every second with the force of 126 trillion horsepower.

But this huge figure amounts to only about one four-billionth of the sun's total emission. Of the rest, some reaches other planets but most is lost in the vastness of space.

Our atmosphere does more than give the earth its weather. In the day it screens out dangerous rays and protects us from too much solar insolation, preventing our burning to a crisp in unbearable heat. At night it is an insulating blanket, blocking outgoing radiation from escape into space.

Differences in radiation absorption account primarily for local heating variations. The oceans, the mountains, the forests, and the flatlands all absorb and radiate heat in numberless differing degrees to affect our climates.

Solar energy, the prime mover of all climatic behavior, is an awesome and impressive force. But it can be manipulated if we understand the principles of radiation—to increase it, decrease it, conserve it, or filter it to better meet our needs.

## Effects of light

The sensitivity of plants to light is illustrated by a flower which opens its petals to the sun by day and closes them tightly at night.

Its effects on the development of green plants are evident through their entire life cycles, however, from germination of the seed through vegetative growth to flowering and fruiting.

Degrees of light intensity are reflected by the type of growth of many plants. If it's bright, short sturdy stems develop. Long thin ones grow under prevailing cloudy conditions. A plant may become misshapen

*Deciduous trees are automatic sun controls. In the summer, the hot sun is screened. During the cold winter, bare branches allow maximum penetration of insolation. Partial foliage in transitional seasons filters the sun.*

*The simple calculator illustrated helps you to closely approximate the noon sun angle from any latitude, during any month of the year. It includes an inner scale divided into months and weeks, and an outer one designating latitude on sun angle.*

*To read it, set the pointer on the inner scale at your latitude. Without moving the pointer, you will see that Los Angeles, latitude 34 degrees, has a maximum sun angle of 79 degrees on the June summer solstice, 33 degrees on the December winter solstice, and 57 degrees on the March and September equinoxes. Placing the pointer at latitude 40 degrees 30', New York has corresponding sun angle readings of 74 degrees, 28 degrees, and 51 degrees. Miami, latitude 26 degrees, reads 87 degrees, 41 degrees, and 65 degrees.*

*At Honolulu, 21 degrees latitude, the June 22 sun is almost directly overhead at 88 degrees above the north horizon, though the minimum sun angle is 47 degrees above the south horizon. (Cities at any distance below that latitude will have to protect against a north mid-day sun, a fact of little consequence to U.S. residents outside of Guam.)*

*When you determine your sun angles, figure the necessary shade protection with a protractor and a scale drawing of your window area. The readings from this simple calculator may not meet the accuracy required by meteorological standards, but are close enough for shading your glass areas satisfactorily.*

## Seasonal sun angles

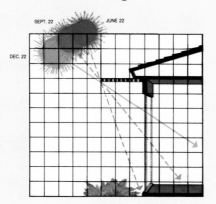

## Sun angle scale

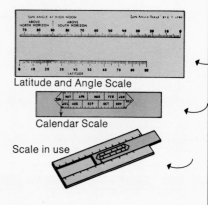

Latitude and Angle Scale

Calendar Scale

Scale in use

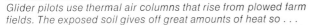

Glider pilots use thermal air columns that rise from plowed farm fields. The exposed soil gives off great amounts of heat so . . .

everytime you grow a seeded lawn or lay sod, you reduce heat radiation. The lawn is always a "climate control" factor.

through its attempts to reach an area of stronger intensity.

Day length is a factor. Some plants grow vegetatively during the long summer days and flower in the fall period of shorter days; in others the cycle is reversed. Some are insensitive to day length.

Plant preferences vary from full sun through several degrees of shade.

Light intensity can be increased by reflection from a light-colored wall or an aluminum foil surface, or by the addition of artificial light in the more controlled environments. It can be moderated to suit particular plant needs by filters of foliage or structure.

## Radiation principles

The sun is the source of the earth's climate. Radiant heat in solar radiation may be either desirable or undesirable, depending upon geographic location, season and air temperature surrounding the recipient.

As light and heat in the form of solar radiation come from the sun, a variety of things occur. Part of it is reflected into space from clouds over the earth; part is scattered and diffused into the

sky vault as it strikes small particles in the earth's atmosphere; and part of it is absorbed by carbon dioxide, water vapor and ozone in the atmosphere. The remainder, approximately one-fifth, penetrates directly through the atmosphere to the earth's surface where it is either absorbed or reflected.

As a result, solar radiation may be received as direct radiation from the sun, as reflected radiation from atmospheric particles found in the sky vault, or as reflected radiation from materials on or near the earth surface.

Trees, shrubs, ground covers and turf are among the best exterior solar radiation control devices. This has been and is one of the major functional uses of plants, both in tropical

climates where solar radiation is oppressive, requiring year-round control, and in temperate climates where solar radiation is most oppressive in summer, requiring seasonal control.

A single plant or a grouping of plants may be used to control direct solar radiation by shading the sun, or by intercepting reflected radiation from some surface. Solar radiation can be intercepted, either before it strikes or after it is reflected, in much the same manner as glare is intercepted.

Plants used for interception of solar radiation may completely block the sun's rays or filter them. Obstruction occurs when plants with dense foliage or multiple layers are used.

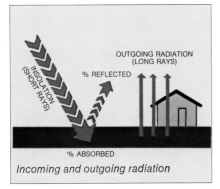

Incoming and outgoing radiation

When the sun goes down, insolation stops and heat loss from the ground begins. Radiation is much faster to a cold high ceiling than a low warm one, and day-night temperatures under them can vary as much as 40 degrees.

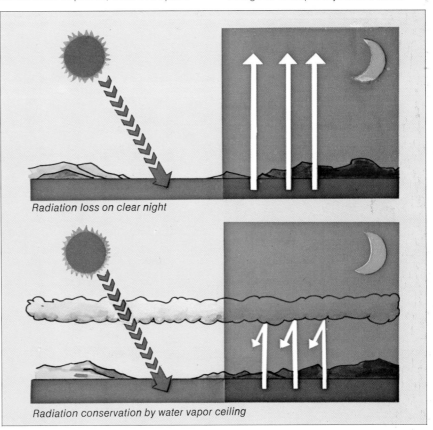

Radiation loss on clear night

Radiation conservation by water vapor ceiling

*Mature trees may require thinning so that the vegetable patch gets full sun.*

*Violets like a cool soil. Here pine bark chips help keep soil cool.*

*Trees in movable containers are expected to shade certain areas of hot marble.*

*A stone mulch not only reflects light but also modifies the soil temperature.*

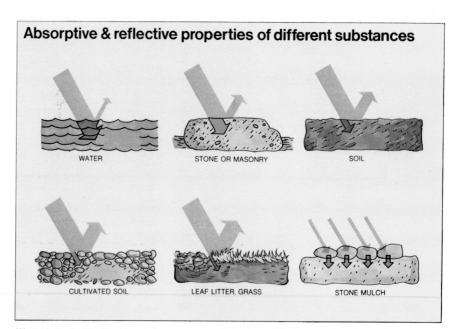

## Absorptive & reflective properties of different substances

WATER · STONE OR MASONRY · SOIL

CULTIVATED SOIL · LEAF LITTER, GRASS · STONE MULCH

*Water is by far the best heat storage reservoir we have. The ocean absorbs 95% of the insolation it receives, reflecting little back into the atmosphere. It is a very slow radiator, and its day and night temperatures are more constant than those of faster radiating land surfaces. The density of granite, and other stone, and masonry, holds their absorption capabilities at higher levels ranging from about 50% to 70%. Average soil absorbs and stores about 30% of the insolation. When cultivated, however, the figure drops to about 20%, as the air spaces created are poor conductors of heat. The capacity of light soil is less than that of dark soil, as light colors reflect more and absorb less than dark ones. The capacities of sand and peat are greater when damp, with their air spaces filled with water. Grass and leaf litter, because of their many air spaces, are at the bottom end of the scale with only 5% storage capacity. Snow is very poor, because of its air content and highly reflective qualities.*

Filtration occurs when plants with open, loose foliage are used.

A tree located to shade the wall and roof in the afternoon will keep house temperatures more comfortable, may reduce the wall and roof temperatures by as much as 20 to 40° Fahrenheit. This helps to eliminate the well-known "attic furnace." Rooftop temperatures of 140 degrees have been recorded. By having a tree shade the west wall and roof of the house you will be protected from the hot sun when and where you most require such protection. Likewise, you can plant different kinds of trees, such as fruit, or other flowering trees around your property to give you shade where you want it, at the time of the year you most desire it.

In the spring, fall and winter, the tree shading your house will not interfere with the sun, which at that time sets in the southwest. Moreover, by use of a tree which sheds its leaves the sun will be certain to shine on the property during the cold season when you need all the natural warmth you can obtain.

Paved areas store and radiate heat for many hours after sundown and may cause stifling conditions in the house at night, making sleep difficult. Plants, on the other hand, transpire and evaporation of the moisture rising from them makes the air cooler.

Noise and dust are absorbed by shrubbery and lawns. A test in one large city revealed that the dust count on the leeward side of a planted area was reduced by 75 per cent.

A solidly paved walk or driveway absorbs as well as reflects heat, and it also causes glare. By making a walk of small squares so that grass grows between them the heat is lowered to considerable extent and glare is reduced.

Patios and swimming pool decks absorb and reradiate a lot of solar energy. Trees and plants in containers can be strategically placed to provide areas of shade. Shade houses—gazebos, garden shelters, teahouses or belvederes—provide an oasis for relaxing or entertaining as well as a a place for growing shade-plants.

The summer solar pattern extends your gardening activity; providing longer growing periods and, exposing to partial sun, areas about the house which are completely shaded in winter. With architectural controls, you can take advantage of the changing sun angle to invite the insolation into the house during the winter and lessen the heating load on your furnace. In the summer, the sun is excluded and your air conditioner is relieved of some of its work.

## Absorption, radiation, and reflection

At night the insolation is shut off, but the ground continues to radiate its heat. Net outgoing radiation is greater than incoming, and the ground cools.

We can use the absorptive qualities of different surfaces to increase their heat storage in chillier climates, or to lessen it in warmer ones.

These qualities are sometimes used for protection during short frost periods, flooding the ground to gain heat from the water and slow outgoing radiation. (The process must be used cautiously, however. Evaporative cooling from sprinkled leaves on damp ground can chill a surface as well.)

By absorbing more insolation during the day, a surface slows down its heat loss at night. This is illustrated on some chilly mornings by frost patches on the grass but not on adjacent soil.

Ground temperatures can be altered through the use of materials with different absorptive properties.

Gardeners, commercial growers, and farmers modify ground conditions with mulches.

Noting the figures on page 36, we can see that cultivation is not necessarily the secret of successful gardening. Many citrus growers in frosty areas never till the soil or shade it with a cover crop.

Marble chips, rocks, or bricks used as decorative mulches around the bases of plants carry more heat to the soil. They are useful for warming effects where higher soil temperatures are desirable.

On the other hand, loose mulches such as grass clipping, leaves, or straw act as an insulation, reducing the solar radiation which reaches soil underneath. In winter this can create a frost problem in cool climates.

Professional growers and farmers are finding plastic film to be a quite satisfactory mulch. Soil temperatures of many acres can be altered, speeding up seed germination and giving higher quantities and qualities of produce. Home gardeners can use plastic on a smaller scale to accomplish the same.

Large surface areas of different substances radiate and reflect solar energy in varying degrees, producing changes in the temperature of the air. Rocky areas, pavements and masonry can create extremely hot mesoclimates in the surrounding

## Differences in reflection by color

*Color affects radiation properties of a surface. More short rays reflect and fewer long rays emit from a light-colored wall; fewer short rays and more long rays from a dark one. Tests on tomatoes show the latter condition results in a leafier plant; the former improves fruiting.*

*Roses thrive against a dark blue wall which absorbs much of the sun's heat.*

*Plants trained against white walls will one day reduce much of the glare.*

environment. At times this can be advantageous as a little sun can be radiated into nearby cold areas, making enjoyable warm sunpockets.

Heat produced by such surfaces in cities is retained by smog and dust and takes a long time to radiate after the sun goes down. Thus city temperatures are higher than the countryside with few radiating areas and cleaner air.

As light surfaces reflect more than dark ones, the color value of a material is another microclimatic control. A wall painted in a high key sends more light to plants near it. Aluminum foil, the best reflector of all, can bounce light into a shady corner to help a plant, or even to give our bodies more even suntans.

When light becomes glare it can be a nuisance, however. A window properly shaded from direct sun can admit reflected rays from light-colored concrete below it. One cure is the substitution of dark paving, flagstone, or brick, but grass would be the best regulator. Though its reflective qualities are high, it is a cool surface and its rough texture diffuses the glare.

*Few places illustrate the need for shade more dramatically than parking lots— a few more trees here would help.*

*To regulate the amount, thin the branches for a more uniform light; prune them higher or narrow to the tree to admit more midday sun.*

*A beautiful planting on the north side of a house. Azaleas enjoy the filtered shade provided by the dogwood tree whose branches have grown toward the sun.*

SUN CONTROL BY DECIDUOUS TREE

*Deciduous trees help cool the house in summer; allow warm sun rays in winter.*

*An example of the principle of summer cooling/winter warming.*

## Radiation control

Moisture in the air, as well as the time of the year, is an important control on the length and type of the growing period. Clouds and fog are widespread and effective insolation controls, and a determining factor of ground temperature and the total amount of light received during the season. Inland Spokane, for example, has greater measurements of both than overcast Seattle.

The differences can decide the types of commercial crops for a region, and whether its gardens are more suitable for foliage or flowering plants.

As clouds are not readily available radiation controls, a tree is a dependable substitute and is shade and can be put where you want it.

If you don't want to hide a view or block air circulation with plantings close to the house, a more remote tree can screen hot sun that is too low for control by your roof overhang. Select a variety whose height will overlap the protection of the overhang.

Obviously, shade trees should be planted on the south and west sides of a building to do the best job of cooling. In colder climates species with compound leaves are especially effective because they have fewer and coarser twigs than those with simply foliage.

There are many ways to make the sun work with you. Shrubbery and lawns may do this, especially by keeping you cooler in summer. The temperature of plants is many degrees cooler than that of pavement in the hot sun. By use of shrubbery and grass the rays of the sun are not reflected against the house from the pavement to make the house doubly hot in summer. Glare, too, is eliminated.

Differences of 8 degrees have been measured on the outer surfaces of shaded and unshaded buildings. Contrasts within are even greater, with differences up to 20 degrees recorded. Heat within an unprotected structure, in fact, can build up to a greater temperature than that outside.

The temperature profiles in the diagrams graphically indicate the cooling potential of shade trees. A single tree on the afternoon side of the house, compared to the unshaded building, can reduce the temperature 10 degrees or more. Planted on the morning side, the tree will delay the heat wave but not diminish it.

Trees with high, arching contours without low growth to impede air circulation about the house, should be selected for shade plantings.

To a lesser degree, climbing and clinging vines also afford summer shade and heat control. They are effective sun screens, supported by trellises, over outdoor areas. Grown on masonry walls, they act as insulating blankets for both hot summer sun and cold winter winds.

"Plant awnings" help to add beauty and graceful living to your home. In the summer time when in full leaf they shade the windows. In winter, providing you use a plant that sheds its leaves, you get the full sun. Either a trellis may be used, or a wire netting close to the house above the window. And for extra measure you can use a vine which provides colorful flowers and adds a splash of brilliance to the house, or even delicious grapes which make the mouth water as they ripen in the fall.

Often we see solid walls of a wood, brick or stucco house out in the sun where they absorb the full blast of the sun's heat. The heat is stored all through the house to cause many sleepless nights. Where this situation exists, vines, shrubs or espaliered plants provide cooler house walls in the summer, and, as with the "plant awnings," if they are the kind that shed their leaves, give the house the full benefit of the sun's warmth in winter.

Espalier trees beside the house walls can also provide delightful blooms and ornamental or edible fruits. If vines are used, they may be colorful, as in the case of climbing roses.

Trellises of plants along one or more walls will add beauty as well as utility. They also give your home an air of graciousness, eliminate that bare look which all home lovers try to avoid. Plants can create a beautiful pictorial effect on your outside walls.

Vines planted against wooden walls can cause deterioration from moisture and make painting or other maintenance difficult. For the same microclimatic effect without the disadvantages, use a vertical trellis to avoid direct contact with the material.

Use deciduous trees and vines when cold seasonal temperatures are a consideration. Their foliage screens hot summer sun, bare branches admit the winter insolation, and screen it during the transitional spring and autumn months.

Barrier plantings have benefits beyond temperature control. They filter out dust, smoke, and other atmospheric impurities. Noise pollu-

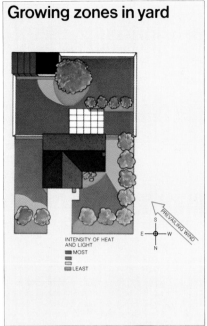

## Growing zones in yard

INTENSITY OF HEAT AND LIGHT
■ MOST
■ 
■ LEAST

*Knowledge of your little climates can open the way to imaginative gardening.*

*Deciduous and fragrant, the azalea mollis likes filtered sun or morning sun.*

*Here many different growing climates can be found in a small area.*

*An attractive north side planting of Japanese aralias and ajuga ground cover.*

*Making the most of a small growing area next to barn-red fence which absorbs much of the sun's heat. Hanging petunias, cabbages, tomatoes trained against the fence, dwarf dahlias and marigolds all co-exist happily.*

# Vertical climates under a shelter

Temperatures change vertically. In the day, ground surfaces are superheated by radiation, compared to air space above. At night, cold air subsides in a chilly layer. Very tender plants in a lath house or patio may fare better on a shelf or in a hanging basket.

In the cool shade of a tunnel-like entrance way, many varieties of begonias find comfort and provide beauty.

Different plants for different types of protection: Top left: Purple wisteria, one of the most useful and beautiful vines provides shade in summer and sunlight in winter. Top right: An arch in Virginia shows wisteria in mid-winter. Bottom left: Dense hedge-like planting of pyracantha stops sun and noise from street. Bottom right: Wispy shade from the weeping willow.

tion, another irritating by-product of industrial progress, can be reduced up to 20 percent by dense thickets of trees and bushes.

In the summer the sun sets in the northwest in the temperate zone and nearer to due west as one goes south. The hottest part of the day is in the early afternoon, when the more direct rays of the sun strike the roof of the house. Later in the afternoon, the rays pour directly on the west wall of the house, heating it to an uncomfortable degree.

## Assessing your microclimates

Many varied microclimatic locations are suitable for different types of plants. Under average weather conditions during a normal growth season, your knowledge of the little climates can help you grow familiar plants better as well as open the way to more imaginative and exotic gardening.

Their variations range from cool north walls, suitable environments for your hardiest plants, to hot-house conditions in a glass enclosure for super-tender varieties.

Your house is a constant climatic regulator, with almost perpetual shade at the north side, full sun and most intense radiation at the south, half shade and hot sun to the west, and half shade with milder sun on the east side. The walls themselves radiate heat to varying degrees; roof overhangs conserve outgoing radiation on frosty nights.

Temperatures change over the flat areas even though exposed to uniform radiation, depending on surfaces of grass, paving, soil, or water. Slopes are miniature banana belts or potential frost zones, according to their direction of pitch.

The lath structure is a controlled area of filtered sun and a moderator of uncomfortable winds.

Under and around the trees are an endless and varying assortment of microclimates. If you can't find one to suit a particular sun and shade requirement, you tailor it with judicious pruning or additional structure.

If prevailing winds are a problem, you can temper them with properly located barriers of plants or structure.

And, if your home is in a hilly area subject to mudslides, anchor your slopes with plantings recommended for the purpose.

## The lawn as energy sink

According to *Scientific American* to grow grass is to engage in a vast struggle against nature. It is fine in damp England, but grass was simply not supposed to grow in many parts of the United States.

Except for the cooling effect of grass as opposed to concrete, a lawn is a classic model of the negative energy system. It takes 162,000 BTUs worth of natural gas to produce the nitrogen in a 50-pound bag of fertilizer. A 10,000 square-foot lawn requires as much as five bags a season. It then takes about half a million or more BTUs worth of gasoline to mow that much lawn and the only product of all this energy input—the grass clippings—is usually thrown away instead of being put to use.

As food shortages continue and prices climb, more Americans will learn to see a vegetable garden as a far more attractive bit of landscaping than grass. Also the garden's taller plants cool things off better and one doesn't throw away its products. Further, the garden provides a need for the grass clippings from whatever lawn area *is* retained: Grass clippings placed between rows of vegetables keep weeds down and fertilize the soil. Commercial growers are using waste materials peculiar to their area, such as Napa Valley grape-pits as mulch.

While you're at it, save the leaves in the fall instead of having them hauled away. With leaves, grass clippings, eggshells, vegetable waste and a little dirt you can start a compost pile which will give you a supply of beautiful humus for the garden.

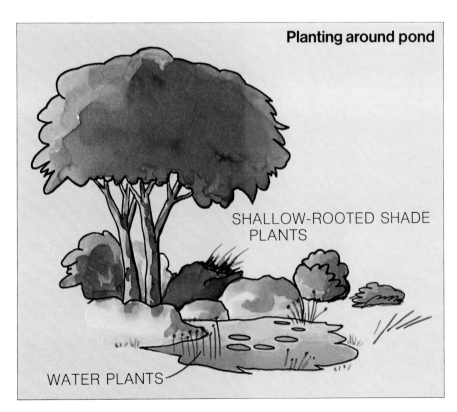

### Planting around pond

SHALLOW-ROOTED SHADE PLANTS

WATER PLANTS

*Planting where there's both shade and water presents special problems and special pleasures. Many exotic plants thrive in this environment.*

*The special rewards of aquatic plants can be seen in this picture.*

The family that owned this yard wanted instant wind protection and privacy. Mature Italian cypress trees took care of both problems.

*Poplars and pines provide good protection from the wind and also give privacy.*

# Harnessing the wind

Here we show some of the numerous ways of modifying the wind to provide you with a better climate.

The location of windbreaks is, of course, the key to their effectiveness. Most cold winter winds throughout the nation come from the North or the West, so windbreaks should be located on those sides, with an extension on the eastern side wherever space permits. The south side should be left open to permit the sun to enter.

In many experiments with anemometers it has been shown that the maximum wind reduction appears at a distance of from four to six times the height of the windbreak, so plantings should be established at this distance from the house. Rapid growing species should be chosen which reach from one to one-and-a-half times the height of the house at maturity.

Based on that kind of calculation, a 20-foot house would benefit most from a hedge of tall evergreen located 80 feet to 120 feet from the north side of the house. A single row of evergreens is effective, but a double or triple row is even more so.

## Increase air circulation

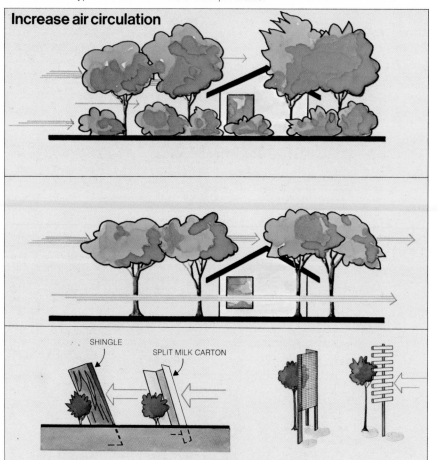

SHINGLE

SPLIT MILK CARTON

Top: Densely packed plants make the house and garden hot and oppressive. Thin them out to allow maximum air circulation. Above left: Shingles pushed into the ground are effective windbreaks for very small plants. Above right: Later, screens of burlap or lath in front of young trees break the force of the wind but permit air circulation. Right: If winds are strong and persistent, young trees need support to prevent up-rooting, breakage, or lopsided growth. Tie them to stakes or frames with cords or flat plastic.

## Support against wind

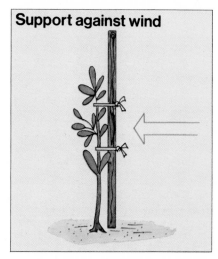

## Multiple braking effect

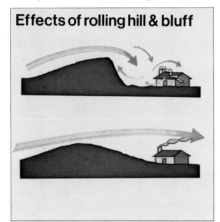

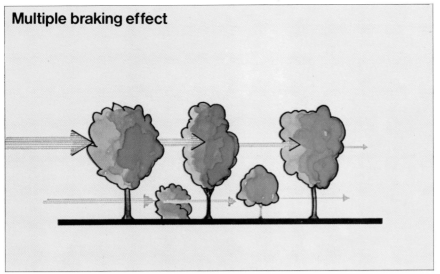

*Multiple rows of trees provide a more effective windbreak than a single row does—each row reduces the wind more completely until it is barely noticeable. To stop the winds nearer the ground plant shrubs beneath the windbreak.*

*Areas such as tennis courts require good windbreaks. Here columnar junipers were used effectively.*

## Effects of rolling hill & bluff

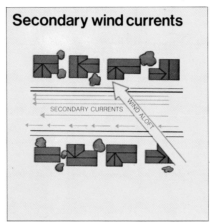

*The abrupt drop of a bluff disrupts smooth air flow, causing swirling eddies, dustiness, and a poor draw in the chimney. Trees between the bluff and the house will reduce the gustiness.*

## Secondary wind currents

SECONDARY CURRENTS

WIND ALOFT

*The wind, crossing the street at an angle, can create secondary currents in a different direction. Stronger on the windward than the leeward side of the street, this condition can be an advantage or a disadvantage.*

## Venturi effect of canyon

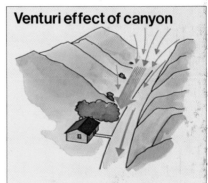

*A house in the bottom of a canyon is subject to stronger diurnal winds than one on flat ground. A breeze can be speeded up by the "venturi" effect of narrow canyon walls, particularly at night.*

## Windbreak protection zones

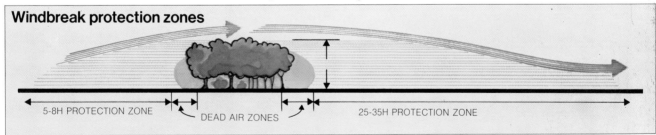

5-8H PROTECTION ZONE — DEAD AIR ZONES — 25-35H PROTECTION ZONE

*The zone of windbreak protection is governed by its size, extending to its leeward from 25 to 35 times its height. The degree of protection diminishes with the distance from the barrier.*
*The windward side is affected as well, with wind speed reduced in a zone 5 to 8 times the height. A narrow band of dead air is immediately in front of the windbreak.*

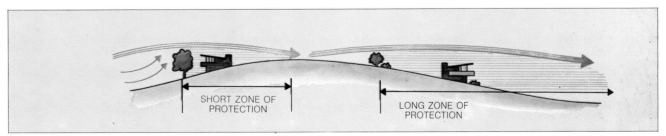

SHORT ZONE OF PROTECTION          LONG ZONE OF PROTECTION

*Slopes modify the length of the protected zones, decreasing them on on the windward side and extending them on the other.*

## Wind effects

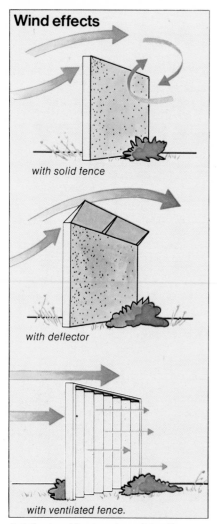

with solid fence

with deflector

with ventilated fence.

A deflector at the top of a solid wall helps smooth the air flow. A more open type fence filters the wind's force.

## Protect tender plants with deflectors...

## or grow them above cold air levels

The structure on the left is used to deflect air flow and protect tender plants. Plants on the right grow above cold air levels.

The old fashioned lattice fence proves to be a good wind modification and allows the neighbors' roses to show through.

Many vines can be trained on large wire mesh screening to provide privacy and attractive protection from the wind.

Two views of a baffle fence which softens the breezes as they pass through it.

Plants edging the path of a breeze help move it a little faster, again the venturi effect. Don't block its channel at the other end of the property with a wall of plants, though, let pass clear through without an impediment.

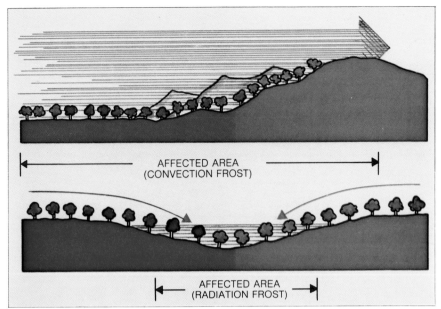

AFFECTED AREA
(CONVECTION FROST)

AFFECTED AREA
(RADIATION FROST)

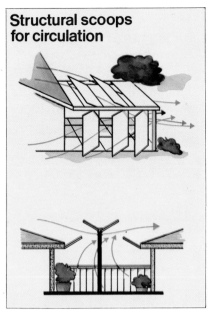

## Structural scoops for circulation

*A big freeze, covering valleys and mountains alike with a frigid blanket, comes by the cold-season movement of a mass of polar air, a common winter occurrence in many regions. Radiation frosts are different, caused by ground heat loss and the patterns followed by cold subsiding air. One area may be affected, a nearby one left untouched.*

*Adjustable scoops, lateral and overhead, deflect breezes into areas when they are most needed or shut off when not.*

# Frost chart

**Hoarfrost.** An accumulation of interconnecting ice crystals formed by the direct conversion of water from vapor to solid. Hoarfrost usually assumes the form of fans, feathers, needles or scales and accumulates on objects such as tree branches, plant stems, leaf edges, poles, wires, etc.

**White frost.** A heavy deposit of hoarfrost.

**Black frost.** A freeze that occurs when the air does not contain enough moisture for the formation of hoarfrost. Freezing of vegetation under such conditions causes plants to blacken or darken.

**Freeze-free season.** The number of days between the last 32° F temperature in spring and the first 32° F temperature in fall.

**Killing frost.** A freeze of sufficient coldness to terminate (or delay the beginning of) the growth of most plants. Since all plants do not suffer permanent injury at the same temperature, the U.S. Weather Bureau ceased using the term in 1948 because of its vagueness. Freezes are now officially defined in terms of 32° F, 28° F, 24° F, 20° F and 16° F or lower. A 32° F or lower freeze occurs when a temperature of 32° F or lower is registered at a height of five feet above ground in an instrument shelter. Similarly, a 16° F or lower freeze happens when a temperature of 16° F or lower is attained.

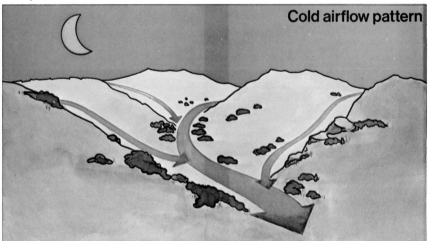

### Cold airflow pattern

*The paths of cold air are easy to predict when you think of it as a liquid. It will follow any natural watershed to its lowest level, where it settles in a pool. When a depression is filled, the air overflows and continues to the next one. The flow increases as the ground continues to lose heat, ceasing only when the morning sun begins a new radiation cycle.*

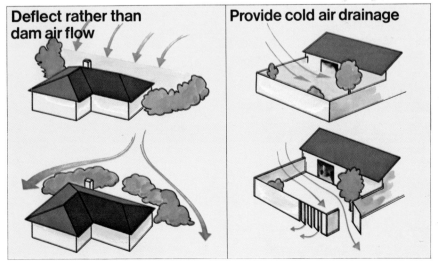

### Deflect rather than dam air flow

### Provide cold air drainage

*Tips to observe in cold weather: Use structure or dense plantings to deflect airflow rather than dam it, as shown on left. Open a gate, or provide other drainage methods in a solid fence enclosing a garden.*

45

## Drainage system for potential trouble areas

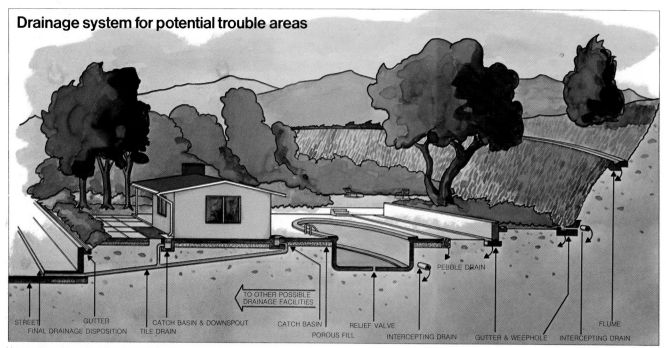

STREET
FINAL DRAINAGE DISPOSITION
GUTTER
TILE DRAIN
CATCH BASIN & DOWNSPOUT
CATCH BASIN
POROUS FILL
RELIEF VALVE
INTERCEPTING DRAIN
PEBBLE DRAIN
GUTTER & WEEPHOLE
INTERCEPTING DRAIN
FLUME
TO OTHER POSSIBLE DRAINAGE FACILITIES

*Uncomfortable and damaging effects and penalties we pay for any kind of land development that alters the original contours and composition of the ground. They may be caused by irregular rainfall patterns, which concentrate heavy downpours and erode the soil; slump, causing saturated soil to slip; limited drainage area, reduced by structure and paving; cut and fill operations, which rearrange existing drainage patterns; and by blockage of natural underground drainage channels by earthfill or structure. Many of these hazards are avoided or controlled on your property by proper drainage systems, which conduct the flows safely to a street or other major outlet.*

# Water in the garden

On a hot, dry summer day, the psychological effects of water are a refreshing boost to our spirits. Dancing reflections from a garden pool, or a cascade tumbling across mossy rocks, remind us of cool lakes and shady mountain brooks.

The mental lift helps, but we receive a more measurable benefit from a microclimatic version of the cooling effect of the ocean on a scorching, dry land mass adjacent to it.

The pond adds water vapor to the air, which can then be cooled by evaporation of the moisture particles which affect your plants, your body, or any other surfaces they touch.

As it evaporates, water borrows heat from the surface during the process. The lower its original humidity, the more additional water vapor it can hold and the greater the potential cooling range. You can measure its degree by comparative readings from wet and dry bulb thermometers, which show the relative air humidity and the modification you can expect from additional saturation.

Plants add to the water vapor in the air by their natural transpiration processes, increasing the humidity available for evaporative cooling.

If the air is near its saturation point already, evaporative cooling potential is reduced. Sprinklers, and transpiring foliage, only add to the humidity. Stepped up air circulation to increase evaporation is the only way to cooler temperatures.

This explains the problems with evaporative type air conditioners in muggy climates, and their reduced efficiency in desert agricultural areas whose humidity has been significantly raised by irrigation and transpiring plants.

Moisture requirements of plants differ. Shallow-rooted varieties need many light irrigations; less frequent but more prolonged watering is necessary to reach the root zones of deeply rooted trees. Some thrive in

*Commercial mist spray installation, by Rain Bird, to cool crops during mid-day heat. System can be easily adapted for home garden use.*

drier soils, others are happier at the bank of a pond.

A general overall soaking at fixed periods is not the best way to schedule irrigation periods. It can apply too much moisture to some plants, not enough to others. Water, a scarce and expensive commodity in some areas, can be wasted.

Limited water availability and the economic facts of successful operation have led modern agriculture to develop more efficient methods of irrigation. Some of these processes are adaptable for your own usage to supplement conventional sprinkling systems and garden hoses.

Most depend on low volume, low-pressure emission to put the water where it's needed and reduce runoff. Heads that spray fan-shaped or circular patterns in adjustable amounts and directions can be spaced at desired intervals along flexible plastic supply lines.

Emitters which release water at a slow steady drip soak the subsoil deeply but leave the surface relatively dry. They are also insertable in plastic lines. These, and other efficient systems, are easily assembled and attach to any available garden valve. Inexpensive pressure regulators and automatic controls add to their versatility.

Telling at a glance when your plants need water, tensiometers inserted into the ground give moisture readings at different underground levels.

But too much underground moisture can be as much a garden problem as too little.

It can create marshy areas, uncomfortable for you and your plants but a delight to the insects of your neighborhood. It can build up destructive hydrostatic pressures behind retaining walls and under swimming pools and paving. It can dislodge a slope, to· spread it over the garden below or crash it against the wall of your home.

You can create more evaporating surfaces by sprinkling the plants, or the wall and roof areas about the house and garden.

Air circulation speeds evaporative processes. You can set up a basic version of an air conditioner with a sprinkler, adjacent to a screen of burlap or other material porous enough to permit penetration by breezes. A fan can provide the circulation on wind-less days.

*Not only do misters lower temperatures but plants thrive in increased humidity. Similar devices have been used by citrus growers as frost defenses in susceptible areas.*

*The home of Frederick Rice, solar energy enthusiast, Palm Springs, California.*

*Mr. Rice studied the weather history in this area, and found that it rarely went without sun for more than 5 days at a time. He uses solar panels (A) on tile roof to heat pool, and mist spray (B) to cool down patio by 8-10 degrees.*

A multitude of chrysanthemums makes this covered patio a special place in the garden. Hanging varieties are suspended from the rafters; standard varieties flank the outside edge. Note the ground cover between the cracks of the patio—this contributes to the cool feeling of the area.

## Special places in the garden:
# Lathhouses, lanais and covered patios

Today's garden is more than just an area for growing plants. It is an extension of the house, for dining and relaxation in pleasant weather, and a center for outdoor activities.

Perfect weather for outdoor comfort, even in the best of climates, is rare. The sun is often too hot in the daytime, evenings become chilly, winds are uncomfortable. Some type of structural controls are necessary additions to get the most from our climates.

Structural outdoor sun shelters are designed in many styles of many materials; are generally uninsulated, and open to air circulation.

If a single roof is insufficient protection against the radiation from fierce sun, shade it with a second roof of canvas or other lightweight material. Allow air circulation between the layers.

A lath shelter is a traditional type of filter to moderate radiation to plants. If you want full shade during midday, a double layer of lath blocks the noon sun but admits it morning and afternoon.

Lath set at an angle will admit milder morning sun but block it in the hot afternoon.

As these will be permanent features, plan them to counteract the prevailing disadvantages. Also consider their effect on the inside climate. A solid patio cover may be a fine summer sunshade, but will it block beneficial winter insolation from the living room?

Bamboo reeding overhead provides just the right amount of sunlight for this collection of exotic plants.

A garden house provides shelter from the sun and a great place for summer entertaining or growing shade plants.

A complete and pleasant "micro-climate" was made in this garden in Florida. The tropical plants thrive in the humidity.

Flexible combinations of climate controls widen the outdoor living range. In a theoretical example for an average condition, the cover retracts or removes for maximum solar exposure in winter. Adjustable screens of glass or plastic block the wind, making the patio a warm sunpocket on clear days. Screens serve the same function in blustery spring or fall weather, the cover is extended for the proper degree of solar regulation. In the summer the cover shades the entire area and a blind drops to block afternoon sun. Screens pivot to catch breezes or may be removed entirely.

The cover may be open at any time to admit daytime radiation to the area, and closed at night to conserve the heat.

Regional conditions, of course, help determine the type of control and the material. A permanent, sloping roof of translucent plastic, with tight glass windscreens, might be recommended in a cool rainy climate, while canvas would serve the purpose in a dry one.

The most suitable arrangement of the control structure will vary with the orientation of your house and the local weather pattern. Unless you're sure of the results, consult an architect before beginning an expensive project.

Surfacing of the outdoor area is important to its heat retention. A paved one will be hotter in the daytime but will re-radiate more heat at night than a wooden one; grass will be cool during daylight and cold at night. Glare is greatest from light colored surfaces.

If evening chill is a problem, a radiant heater installed in the floor will help.

A brazier or portable radiant heater also warms an outdoor area. Locate it so warmth is reflected back to you from walls and ceilings, rather than lost to the air.

The monumental stone or brick barbecue pits, which used to be massive features of the outdoor cooking centers, have been largely replaced by lightweight portable models.

Locate yours downwind to carry away its smoke, in a spot where it can't damage overhead foliage or roof overhang.

It's best to be upwind also from a pond, marsh or other site which might breed insects. Amber lights attract fewer of the little pests than white ones. If they're a serious problem you may have to enclose the outdoor living area with screens.

You can put the weather to work for you in your swimming pool. Solar heaters are available which warm and circulate the water. Water temperatures are maintained better if the surface is covered at night with plastic sheets to block outgoing radiation. In southwestern desert areas some pools are equipped with a fine spray of water to cool the overheated water and air by evaporation.

Here's a good idea from the American Association of Nurserymen.

"Where wind is a problem in the enjoyment of a garden, and you still may not want to cut off the view, oftentimes a combination of hedges and glass will solve your difficulty. Especially is this true where you do not wish to shut off a view of a river, lake, ocean, valley, or other natural vista. One or more windows of

*An area especially designed for the fern and tuberous begonia buff. The lath overhead protects these tender plants from the direct afternoon sun.*
*The planting area was filled with a special light-weight soil mix to pamper prize-winning begonias.*

*A lath enclosure not only provides a pleasant place for plants; tired gardeners find comfort there too!*

*An outside view of the lath house at left. This one gets multiple use as potting shed, tool storage area, summer eating place and fern "grotto." Cabinets and special soil bins were built in. Note the compost bin to the left.*

*This patio in Florida, covered with a roof of fiberglass panels, gets maximum use through much of the year. The soft diffused light and the protection from the wind and rain make it an ideal growing area and meeting place.*

glass constructed with a wind-breaking hedge on each side, can be a very striking addition to the outdoor garden which otherwise cannot be enjoyed because of cold winds. One of the great advantages of this treatment is that, by trapping the sun, it also enables you to use the garden in the late spring and early fall.''

Eddies can be a nuisance in a patio sheltered by the solid house, but a few plants within it can break them up. Plants may even be grown in movable planters, adjustable to different wind conditions. Also, eddies can be controlled with an overhead canopy of either lath or solid structure.

The eddy behind a solid wall is similar to that behind the bluff. A deflector at its top helps smooth airflow.

A more open type fence, slotted or picket style, filters the wind through to reduce its force without the eddy.

*Plastic roller shades shield a covered patio from sunlight and wind and create instant climatic changes.*

*A family greenhouse in Ventura, Calif. provides complete climate control. Lath roof protects against too much sun.*

*Roses bloom along the path leading to an impressive lath house - greenhouse combination in a small back yard.*

# Conservation of energy through proper planting

Written by: Erick Katzmaier

Here's an example of growing native plants in California. It can be adapted to any state.

Conservation of energy is important to every aspect of our lives. Garden practices, soil preparation and plant selection are important parts of life on our earth and can be a significant factor in the wise conservation of energy.

Selection of native plants for gardening or landscaping is a wise beginning toward resource conservation. Plants that grow naturally in an area are suited to the region's amount of rain, wind, snow or soil. This means that native plants withstand these conditions with fewer requirements for spraying, feeding, pruning or watering. A small project undertaken in the Silverlake area of Los Angeles will give one example of this idea.

A southwest slope of clay and decomposing granite had been unplanted for years. It was weed covered and needed attention. One gallon-size California natives were selected and planted. No soil amending was done. Holes slightly larger and deeper were prepared. After planting, each plant was given one gallon of water once a month. Planting was done prior to the winter and spring rains, thereby taking advantage of a natural water requirement of these plants.

Selections for this area were, Fremontia Californica, Flannel Bush, a beautiful yellow flowered shrub, Ceanothus thrysiflorus and cyaneous, both spectacular blue flowering shrubs, Zauschneria Californica, a low shrub with gray foliage and bright orange blossoms, Pinus radiata, Monterey Pine, Pinus coulteri Coulter, pine, Heteromeles arbutifolia, the brilliant Christmas Berry and Washingtonia filifera, Fan Palm. All of these plants grew. Some did better than others. They are growing in a manner appropriate to the California climate. Following the spring rains the plants produce dense lush growth, resplendent in spring. As the natural dryness of summer approaches, the plants trim their foliage and adjust to the heat and lack of water. It seems that 50% of the leaves fall from the plants in order to help control transpiration. In spite of this, they retain their beauty,

more appropriately, it seems, because they fit the seasons.

Another planting of California natives was in Laguna Beach. This was different in many respects. It was subject to coastal moisture and was near a garden, thereby receiving more water and care.

Seeds of coastal wildflowers were sown in a prepared bed. One gallon-size Coreopsis gigantea, the brilliant yellow daisy like coastal bluffs plant, Coreopsis maritima, Golden yarrow, and several forms of Sedum were added to the bed. A Matilija poppy (Romneya coulteri) was added while still remaining in its can. Its roots are sensitive and, to insure success in planting, it is best to punch holes in the can and plant can and plant together. A clump of blue-eyed grass (Sisyrinchium bellum) and Columbine (Aquilegia eximia) were planted beneath the taller plants. This collection comprised this coastal flower bed.

Soil in Laguna is heavy. Preparation of the bed included removal of 12 inches of soil and mixing it with about 60% river sand. After planting, the flowers received once-a-week lawn sprinkling for the first 6 months. Adjacent non-native flowers developed mildew and were more susceptible to snails, slugs and aphids.

By the latter part of the year the native plants had covered this particular bed. The plants touched each other and shaded the soil beneath them. This resulted in a better rate of growth and a lesser demand for water. Currently the plants receive water once a week for less than a minute. The flowers are profuse and the plants healthy.

Seasonal fog supplements the watering. The plants at Silverlake, during similar seasons, were dryer. The plants adjust to this difference by methods previously mentioned. They still are beautiful, healthy specimens.

The point to be made out of this is that beautiful gardens, rich in color, whether evergreen or deciduous, can be achieved with natives. This end can be reached with minimal watering, soil preparation and maintenance.

Natives requiring more moisture respond very well to mulching. The Huntington Beach Parks Department has been applying mulch to their parks for several years. Most recently, applications have been made to their largest park, Central Park. The soil of Central Park varies considerably. There are sandy soils, heavy soils, ones high in peat and others in salt. A careful plant selection was made to introduce plants able to tolerate these conditions. Cuttings were taken of

existing trees on the site. Grass was matched to that already found growing.

Following the planting a mulching program began. Four to 6 inches of mulch was applied in planting beds. This consisted of tree trimming chips, mushroom compost, and stable manure.

The trees and shrubs which were generally planted as gallon-size plants (24″ in height maximum) began to respond. The Alders, Eucalyptus and California peppers grew the fastest. After a year many of these trees had reached 8 feet in height. Their growth, besides being rapid, has produced healthy, well-developed trees.

Water for these plants and lawn is supplied by an automatic system. It operates once every 2 or 3 days. Because of the mulch the soil does not become hard and dry. Instead it maintains a more constant moisture level. It is also being enriched by the decomposition of mulch and the addition of beneficial bugs and worms in the soil. What was once hard soil is beginning to become lighter, more viable soil.

A smaller application of mulch, produced from a backyard compost pile, produced satisfying results. Water would not penetrate soil in a small garden plot in Los Angeles. A composted mulch of 2 to 3 inches was applied for 4 to 6 months. The water began to enter the soil and the soil began to lighten. In about a year it was possible to dig into a few inches of the soil with one's hand. There was also evidence that earthworms were again prevalent. The resulting effect was healthy plants and beautiful blooms. The plants also became more resistant to insects. These small creatures were still in the garden but the healthy plants had developed a resistance to them.

The work done in these projects illustrates some of the advantages of proper plant selection, soil preparation and maintenance. It has been shown that a great expenditure of resources is not necessary to produce beautiful gardens. If we take what is around us and build our gardens from these indigenous materials we will produce beautiful gardens appropriate to the environment in which we live. Through efforts of this kind we will work and achieve a real conservation of energy.

For additional information on growing native plants contact your state Cooperative Extension Office; arboretums or gardens in your area, or professional landscape architects or nurserymen.

# Growing in an indoor climate

We humans are able to move freely through our homes, to put on or remove a sweater or a blanket, to find or create a more comfortable micro-climate. Plants, lacking this mobility, are dependent on us for their needs. They must be located carefully in zones most favorable to their health when brought inside.

When planting in the ground the basic problem of finding the right place for the plant, or vice versa, is generally a one-time decision. But, with potted plants you have the chance to second guess yourself as often as you like, or as often as you and the plant can tolerate. In this interaction between yourself and a pot of greenery you may learn a lot about the plant, and even more about yourself. You may turn out to be a true plants person; with parsley and chives in the living room and a giant philodendron that takes over the kitchen. On the other hand, decoration may be your thing, and you put a plant where it makes the room look best and toss it out when it becomes unhappy.

Most of us will fall somewhere in between; we will try to find the right plant for a particular place, and the place with just the right conditions for a particular plant. Location isn't every-thing, but without it—the right soil mix, a perfect watering schedule and all the rest of your loving care will avail very little.

We are not always aware of the tremendous variations possible in the indoor microclimates. Many factors, natural and man-made, can produce highly localized little weathers rang-ing from tropic heat to arctic frigidity, gloomy overcast to desert glare, all within a 24 hour period.

The average modern house is too hot and too dry for most plant culture. An indoor gardener must be alert to the need of finding or creating the

◁

*A bay window provides excellent light for many houseplants. Outdoor hanging baskets can be brought indoors when desired.*

most favorable growth conditions, and avoiding or correcting those which are detrimental.

Plants and humans respond in similar ways to the weather. Both feel better in cooler, moister, well-ventilated rooms than in overheated, stuffy, bone-dry ones. If you are uncomfortable in any particular spot, your plant probably feels the same way about it.

Temperature, light intensity and ventilation determine whether indoor plantings thrive or wither. Preliminary study of their requirements and the conditions of your home can indicate the increase or reduction of the factors necessary for successful cultivation.

You may be able to brighten some rooms with flowering plants, or might be restricted in others to leathery-leaved old reliables whose tolerance to unfavorable conditions was proven years ago in dim Victorian corners.

Don't expect too much from this type gardening. Plant characteristics change; a fruiting variety may never be able to produce more than foliage or flowers indoors.

The more controllable indoor climates can produce a more uniform growth pattern throughout the United States. You can reproduce a tiny section of the climate of virtually any spot on the map. Exterior weather will have an effect on the way you tend your plants, however. Less irrigation is needed in rainy Seattle than arid Phoenix; the amount of solar ex-posure or protective screening varies the intensity of the sun or the season at a particular locality.

## Temperature and light

The effects of these important factors on plant growth are closely related. The higher the light intensity, the more heat a plant can stand.

Night-time temperatures, therefore, should be cooler than those of the day. Most house plants prefer 50 to 60 degrees after dark, some like it as cool as 35 degrees (only a few can tolerate, without wilting, the 70 degrees human comfort range). Their daytime tolerances average about 15 degrees above those of night in sunny weather, 10 degrees if cloudy.

Light requirements vary with the plant. Some do best in full sunlight, others want it part of the day only. Many prefer diffused light to direct sun. See accompanying chart for specific suggestions.

Too little light is one of the most common microclimatic deficiencies. Unless a room or corner is bright enough to read the telephone book, do needlepoint, or take a photograph, your plant will have a hard time. (Don't be misled in your plant selec-tion by those flourishing in a dim restaurant or hotel lobby—they may be provided by a plant service and periodically replaced.)

Usually, foliage plants need light only; flowering varieties need the solar exposure as well. Requirements for propagation or early growth may also differ from those for mature plant maintenance.

*Plants in this sunken garden all love humidity and sub-tropical warmth. Species needing the most light are placed nearest the window.*

# Plants for a sunny location

Very few plants can thrive in full, direct sunlight all day. Plants listed below need at least 5 hours of direct sunlight in winter. In areas where there is much snow, remember that rays of sun bouncing from snow can add up to 30 per cent additional light. Also white painted buildings or expanses of unshaded land can increase available sunlight. Gardeners in southern and western sunshiny states may find windows with southern and eastern exposures too bright for plants other than some cacti and other succulents. In other areas, southern or eastern exposures provide the required light for these plants. All the plants listed here will thrive in average house temperature and a slightly moist (humidity 30%) atmosphere.

**Bulbs**

| | |
|---|---|
| Agapanthus* | Hyacinth* |
| Amaryllis* | Ixia* |
| Anemone* | Montbretia* |
| Caladium | Oxalis* |
| Calla lily* | Ranunculus* |
| Daffodil* | Tulbaghia* |
| Freesia* | Tulip* |
| Haemanthus* | |

**Flowering plants**

| | |
|---|---|
| Begonia | King's crown |
| Bird-of-Paradise | Lilies |
| Chrysanthemum | Miniature rose |
| Geranium | Passion flower |
| Gerbera | Poinsettia |
| Gloriosa | Shrimp plant |

**Foliage plants**

| | |
|---|---|
| Agave* | Herbs |
| Aloe* | Iresine |
| Aporocactus* | Jerusalem cherry |
| Astrophytum* | Joseph's coat |
| Bamboo | Kalanchoe* |
| Beaucarnea | Lobiva* |
| Caphalocereus | Mammillaria* |
| Coleus* | Notocactus* |
| Crassula | Opuntia |
| Echeveria* | Pereskia* |
| Echinocactus | Polyscias |
| Echinocereus* | Rebutia* |
| Echinopsis* | Saxifraga |
| Eucalyptus | Sedum |
| Euphorbia* | Stapelia* |
| Fatshedera | Stone plants* |
| Gymnocalycium* | Wax plant* |
| Gynura | |

**Shrubs**

| | |
|---|---|
| Acalypha* | Ixora* |
| Allamanda* | Myrtle* |
| Azalea* | Nandina |
| Bougainvillea* | Oleander* |
| Citrus* | Pittosporum* |
| Coccoloba | Privet* |
| Croton | Pyracantha* |
| Flowering maple* | Rhododendron* |
| Gardenia* | Silk oak |
| Hibiscus* | Stephanotis* |
| Hydrangea* | Sweet olive* |

*Also produces significant flowers.

# Plants for a semi-sunny location

Plants suggested in this category need 2 to 5 hours of sunlight in winter. In warm weather, they will do well in bright light with little or no direct sun. Provide a warm (60- to 80-degree), slightly moist (humidity 30% or more) atmosphere. These plants can be grown in an area that receives full sun if they are protected by a curtain, or if a sun-loving plant rises up to give some shade. In summer they do well in bright light with little or no direct sun. Most exposures fit this category, except those facing north or south. Also this seems to be the preferred lighting for a large portion of jungle-oriented tropical plants. Many of the flowering plants listed in the Sunny category can bloom in this light with additional light reflected from white buildings or open spaces outside.

**Bulbs**

| | |
|---|---|
| Caladium | Hyacinth* |
| Clivia* | Narcissus* |
| Daffodil* | Tulip* |

**Flowering plants**

| | |
|---|---|
| Achimenes | Flame violet |
| African violet | Gloxinia |
| Calceolaria | Impatiens |
| Christmas cactus | King's crown |
| Cineraria | Lipstick vine |
| Crossandra | Orchids |
| Cyclamen | Shrimp plant |

**Foliage plants**

| | |
|---|---|
| Asparagus | Liriope* |
| Beaucarnea | Norfolk Island Pine |
| Begonia* | Palms |
| Brassaia | Pandanus |
| Bromeliads* | Pellionia |
| Chlorophytum | Peperomia |
| Cissus | Philodendron |
| Coleus | Pilea |
| Columnea* | Pleomele |
| Crassula | Pothos |
| Cyperus | Prayer plant* |
| Dizygotheca | Rhipsalis |
| Dracaena | Rhoeo* |
| Euphorbia* | Saxifraga |
| Fatsia | Snake plant |
| Fatshedera | Spathiphyllum* |
| Ferns | String-of-pearls |
| Ficus | Swedish ivy |
| Fittonia | Syngonium |
| Gynura | Tolmiea |
| Haworthia | Tradescantia |
| Hypoestes | Wax plant* |
| Ivy, English | Zebra plant* |
| Joseph's coat | Zebrina |

**Shrubs**

| | |
|---|---|
| Ardisia* | Fuchsia* |
| Aucuba | Gardenia* |
| Camellia* | Nandina |
| Clerodendrum* | Pittosporum* |
| Coffea* | Podocarpus |
| Dipladenia* | Silk oak |
| Eleagnus* | Sweet olive* |
| Euonymus | Tibouchina* |
| Ficus | |

*Also produces significant flowers.

# Plants for a semi-shady location

Plants in this group thrive in bright, open light, but need little or no direct sunlight. They will succeed in a warm, slightly moist atmosphere. Most are grown primarily for foliage.

**Bulbs**

Caladium

**Flowering plants**

| | |
|---|---|
| Achimenes | Flowering tobacco |
| African violet | Impatiens |
| Christmas cactus | Orchids |

**Foliage plants**

| | |
|---|---|
| Acorus | Ivy, English |
| Anthurium | Liriope* |
| Asparagus | Norfolk Island pine |
| Aspidistra | Palms |
| Begonia* | Pandanus |
| Brassaia | Pellionia |
| Bromeliads* | Peperomia |
| Chinese evergreen | Philodendron |
| Cissus | Pilea |
| Dracaena | Pothos |
| Dieffenbachia | Prayer plant* |
| Ferns | Selaginella |
| Ficus | Snake plant |
| Helxine | Spathiphyllum* |
| Hypoestes | Syngonium |

**Shrubs**

| | |
|---|---|
| Ficus | Podocarpus |
| Pittosporum | |

*Also produces significant flowers.

# Plants for shaded locations

Many foliage plants will grow in an area that receives no sunlight. But there should be enough light to cast a shadow when you pass your hand across the area in which the plant will be placed. It's a good idea to rotate plants kept in poor light—give them a week or two of bright light, even 2 hours of morning sunlight, then let them have a sojourn in the dimly lighted place.

**Foliage plants**

| | |
|---|---|
| Asparagus | Ivy, English |
| Aspidistra | Liriope |
| Chlorophytum | Palms |
| Chinese evergreen | Philodendron |
| Cyperus | Pothos |
| Dieffenbachia | Selaginella |
| Dracaena | Snake plant |
| Ferns | Spathiphyllum* |
| Ficus | Syngonium |

**Shrubs**

| | |
|---|---|
| Ficus | Podocarpus |
| Pittosporum | |

*Also produces significant flowers.

# Fresh air and moisture

The drafty construction and chilly, high-ceilinged rooms of the old-fashioned farmhouse may not have done much for the comfort of its human occupants, but the quantity of fresh moist air they admitted created plant-growing opportunities unequalled by today's tight, centrally heated homes.

Excessive atmospheric humidity is rarely a problem. As well as irrigating their roots, the gardener must constantly check and supplement plants' needs for a moister climate in their surrounding atmosphere.

Fresh air also is necessary to raise local humidity and perk up the plants. To avoid damage to them, however, it must be brought in carefully from the outside. Locate plants where they will receive ventilation, but away from direct blasts, drafts, or air cold enough to chill them. (See illustrations, p. 61.)

House plants are often set outside to receive the benefits of a gentle rain, or to lower their respiration rate from that of an overheated room. Be careful of shock from too hot sun to tender tissues, or, in cold weather, from chilling. A covered porch shades them, or conserves radiation during low temperatures.

# Assessing your microclimates

An indoor gardener must weigh the cumulative effect of *all* microclimatic factors to determine what species he can grow, and where to locate them. In an average home, he will probably find a favored spot in almost every room (though it may be restricted to foliage types).

Plants usually flourish in the kitchen. It is well lighted naturally and artificially; sinks and steaming pots keep humidity higher than that of the rest of the house.

Additional moisture from faucets and tubs also makes the bathroom a good location if well lighted.

Unless draperies are pulled to protect furniture from the sun, the living room usually has the advantage of good exposure and light conditions. It is most subject to dryness and overheating, however, so guard against dryness and poor ventilation.

A lower average temperature than the rest of the house is a favorable point for the bedroom. Don't cut beneficial light during the day with tightly closed draperies. Upstairs rooms,

particularly, are well located above the tops of most outdoor plants where they receive maximum solar exposures and air circulation.

Serious gardeners often drape windows with plants, both tree-sized and container varieties. The room is shaded while plants enjoy the sun. Select species suitable for the amount of light available. See chart on page 56.

Skylights and windows near the ceiling widen your choice of plant locations.

Basements are cool, but dark. They are better used for propagating than growing. Gro-lights increase usefulness of area. A fan may be needed for air circulation.

As conditions vary so rapidly in such a short distance, a thermometer, a hygrometer for moisture readings and a photographic light meter will help keep tabs on the changing microclimates of your home.

A quick plant/light inventory inside our house shows a range of plants that seem quite happy in locations with light intensities from 64-foot candles up to 8000. Not too surprisingly the plant locations outside the house cover essentially the same intensity range. However, it is hard to find a place outside the house that falls below 64-foot candles on a bright day, while most of the interior is below that level. From this it is apparent that our indoor and outdoor plants are interchangeable; at least when the temperatures and other conditions are compatible. Of course the winter sun is less intense, the day length shorter, and the number of days of full sun during summer and winter would seem to present an even greater variable. Summer fog in some coastal regions may cut the total possible sunshine by 50%; while rains and overcast may cut the total possible sunshine by 50%, amount in other areas.

While overcast days drastically reduce the amount of light falling on plants in direct sunlight situations, they do not necessarily reduce the illumination on plants in a window situation where they receive their light from the sky. In fact, the light intensity in such an indoor situation may be more than twice as bright on an overcast or bright cloudy day as it is on a clear day, when the illumination comes from a deep blue sky.

A simple light meter or a camera with a built in meter can be used to make an illumination inventory of your house. If your meter only gives you an exposure setting, set the film speed at ASA 100 and aim the

meter at a white card placed to approximate the position of the plant leaf surface. The shutter speed reading (taken as a whole number) that will appear opposite f4 will correspond to the approximate foot candles of illumination—i.e. if the indicated exposure is 1/250 sec. at f4 this will be 250-foot candles.

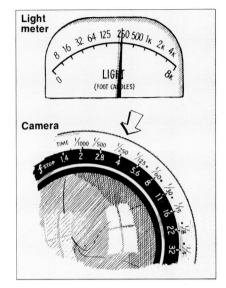

If you take an illumination inventory of your house you are likely to discover that there are many areas where you would like to have plants that are at the low end of the light scale. In many houses the only areas with light intensity above 250-foot candles are the window sills themselves; except of course where the direct sun shines in and abruptly pushes it up to 8000 or more. 250-foot candles is about the same as the illumination 1 foot away from a 100 watt bulb in a reflector. 8000-foot candles is great for the eggplant in your vegetable garden but likely to cook your asparagus fern.

*Pandanus, or screw pine, is usually classified as one of the indestructibles.*

# Approximate foot-candles by location

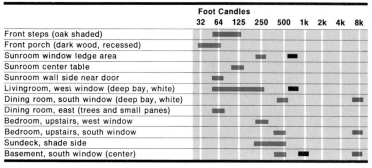

| Location | Foot Candles 32 · 64 · 125 · 250 · 500 · 1k · 2k · 4k · 8k |
|---|---|
| Front steps (oak shaded) | |
| Front porch (dark wood, recessed) | |
| Sunroom window ledge area | |
| Sunroom center table | |
| Sunroom wall side near door | |
| Livingroom, west window (deep bay, white) | |
| Dining room, south window (deep bay, white) | |
| Dining room, east (trees and small panes) | |
| Bedroom, upstairs, west window | |
| Bedroom, upstairs, south window | |
| Sundeck, shade side | |
| Basement, south window (center) | |

▬ Clear day — Blue sky
▬ W/Morning high fog
▬ Direct sunlight

# Illumination requirements for plants

*This chart was compiled from data from a number of different sources and is generally based on 12 hours a day of light at a fixed intensity. Those plants shown with ranges extending to 8000 foot candles will generally take some full sun. In window planting situations it is important to provide sufficient ventilation to prevent excessive heat build-up even with plants that can thrive on direct sun exposure.*

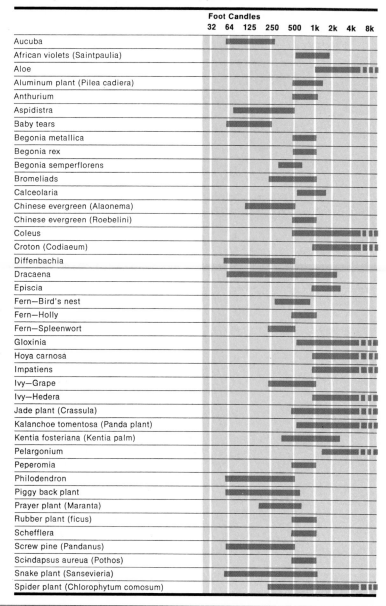

| Plant | Foot Candles 32 · 64 · 125 · 250 · 500 · 1k · 2k · 4k · 8k |
|---|---|
| Aucuba | |
| African violets (Saintpaulia) | |
| Aloe | |
| Aluminum plant (Pilea cadiera) | |
| Anthurium | |
| Aspidistra | |
| Baby tears | |
| Begonia metallica | |
| Begonia rex | |
| Begonia semperflorens | |
| Bromeliads | |
| Calceolaria | |
| Chinese evergreen (Alaonema) | |
| Chinese evergreen (Roebelini) | |
| Coleus | |
| Croton (Codiaeum) | |
| Diffenbachia | |
| Dracaena | |
| Episcia | |
| Fern—Bird's nest | |
| Fern—Holly | |
| Fern—Spleenwort | |
| Gloxinia | |
| Hoya carnosa | |
| Impatiens | |
| Ivy—Grape | |
| Ivy—Hedera | |
| Jade plant (Crassula) | |
| Kalanchoe tomentosa (Panda plant) | |
| Kentia fosteriana (Kentia palm) | |
| Pelargonium | |
| Peperomia | |
| Philodendron | |
| Piggy back plant | |
| Prayer plant (Maranta) | |
| Rubber plant (ficus) | |
| Schefflera | |
| Screw pine (Pandanus) | |
| Scindapsus aureua (Pothos) | |
| Snake plant (Sansevieria) | |
| Spider plant (Chlorophytum comosum) | |

The flexibility of plant placement within a room will be dictated by the size and number of windows and the brightness of the walls. The light intensity very close to a small window will be very much the same as it is with a large window. However, as we move away from the small window the intensity decreases more rapidly. Three feet away from a large window wall the light intensity may still be half as bright as it was 6 inches from the window.

If you have one or more large south windows that receive full winter sun for most of the day you can:

✔ grow a small vegetable and herb garden all winter, even a big zucchini in a rolling tub.

✔ maintain a small avocado tree or citrus through the winter; wheel it outside for the summer.

✔ keep a minimum maintenance garden of cacti and succulents.

✔ force daffodils into bloom for Christmas.

✔ in the spring you can use it to get an early start on garden vegetables or annual flowers.

North windows are pretty much limited to the indoor foliage plants on a permanent basis although lots of others will get along if given recovery periods in brighter light. North light is uniform and dependable and when supplemented with artificial sources it will do almost anything you might want.

Eastern and western windows may provide from 2 to 4 hours of direct sunlight, enough to get good color from coleus, and bloom from impatiens and gloxinia. Croton, osmanthus, campanula should do well. Remember that there is a lot of difference between two hours of early morning sun and four hours of strong afternoon sun.

# Comparative microclimates

Architectural design, construction, and orientation govern the favorable plant zones in a house. Full walls of glass, naturally, provide more usable areas than scattered small windows. But you can find some suitable climates in any building through spot comparisons.

When summer sun is high, direct radiation through a window can burn plants. A thermometer behind the glass can read 140 degrees, though the rest of the room is comfortable.

## Seasonal exposures

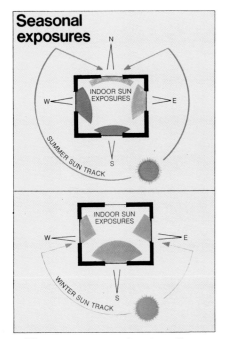

Winter rays are weaker, traveling a longer distance through the atmosphere, and plants seldom need protection from the sun.

At its low winter angle, the sun reaches farther into the room, increasing the size of the zone in which a plant receives light from a single window.

*Reduce the sunlight entering a room to the advantage of the Plant. Plant A receives light at its base where it does no good. A shade operating from the bottom gives plant B the same amount of light, but on the leaves where the plant benefits.*

## Placement of light

## Comparative light meter readings
### (Summer, 2:30 p.m.)

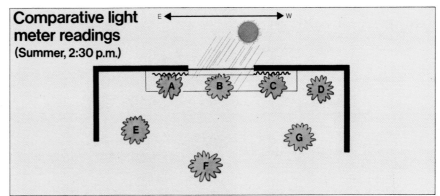

*Meter readings of noon light intensities. Plants A, C and D, out of direct sun receive a fraction as much as B. E, F and G gain some light reflected from the floor and other surfaces. A and C, however, receive direct sun for parts of day.*

## Summer heat & light intensities

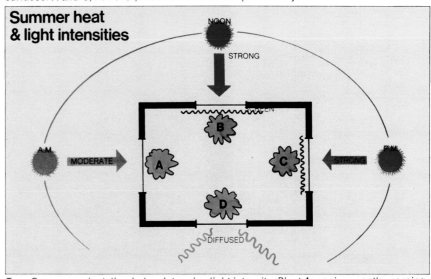

*Top: Compass orientation helps determine light intensity. Plant A receives gentle morning sun, seldom needs protection from it. B, in full sun most of the day, needs most summer shelter. C receives partial sun only, but may require shading from harsh afternoon rays.*
*Bottom: Plants reach toward the light source. A, in the far corner of an unevenly lit room, grows weak and stringy. B, with better balanced light from several sources, stands more chance of developing into a strong, well shaped plant. A skylight helps it even more.*

## Balanced light

*Plants set up their own microclimates. A in direct sun, B in full shade under broadleafed D, and C in the filtered light.*

## Climates for different plants

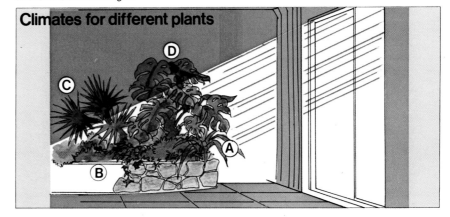

## Light control by architecture

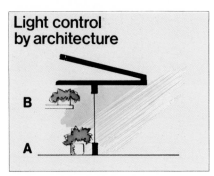

External architectural features influence the light received through a window. Above, high plant B is shaded by the overhang, while the lower position of A benefits from the sun.

## Light control by tree

If not too dense, outdoor trees are effective filters for too-strong sun. A deciduous tree, leafless in winter, admits almost full sun when it is most needed.

## Light control by location of outside tree

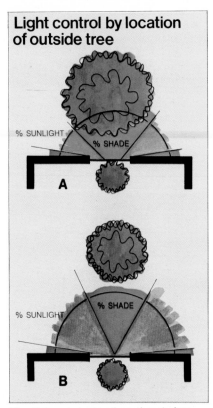

The distance of a tree from the window regulates the total light an indoor plant receives. Near a window, it cuts most of the intensity of solar energy from A, while B is shaded only a small percentage of the time.

## Outside tree and solar intensity

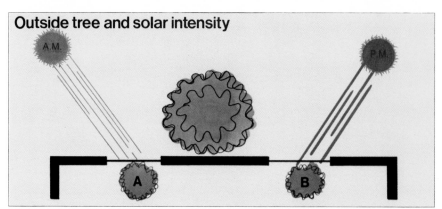

Compass orientation affects the type of light a tree admits to a room. A, a good location for more tender plants, has mild morning sun only. Hardier varieties tolerate the strong afternoon radiation at B.

## Light reflected off wall

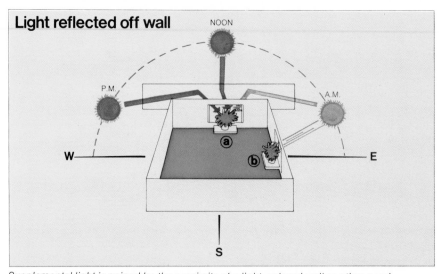

Supplemental light is gained by the proximity of a light-colored wall or other good reflecting surface. Though never in direct sun, the total light bounced off the wall the entire day, at A, can equal that of B, with morning exposure only.

## Overcast vs. clear skies

While residents of the rainy northwest and smoggy cities keep plants next to windows for whatever sun they can get, those in sunnier climates have to provide protection from the direct rays of the sun.

Plants requiring good light are placed near high windows in this Hawaiian home. At the floor level are tropicals which thrive in low light. Humidity is increased by grouping plants like this.

## Vertical differences

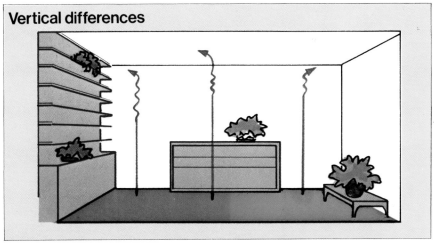

Rising heated air creates vertical microclimates, varying as much as 10° from floor to ceiling. Temperature range varies, of course, according to the size, construction, and heating method of the room. Lower positions, receiving more light and less heat, are usually the more favored plant zones.

## Light reflection on varied surfaces

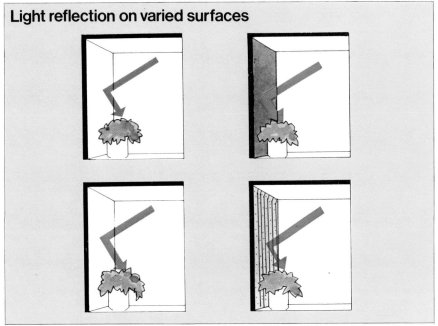

Varying light intensities are reflected by different wall surfaces. A white wall reflects up to 10 times as much as a dark one, which absorbs most of the rays. Though their color may be the same, a smooth surface is a better reflector than a draped or rough-textured one.

## Insulated vs. uninsulated walls.

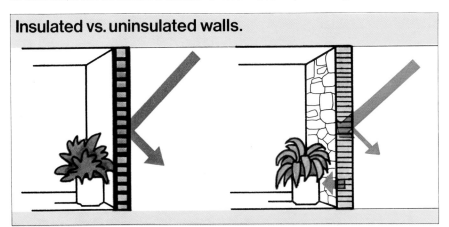

Uninsulated walls are uncomfortable in hot weather. Radiated heat supplements normal conditions, and continues long after sundown when plants need lower temperatures. The increase may be 15 or 20° behind the wall, but decreases rapidly with distance. South and west walls are the hottest, poor locations for plants immediately adjacent to them.

## Supplementary light

Artificial light from reading and work lamps can supplement daylight after sundown. Intensity is greatest nearest the light source: A and B are both in the direct beam of the lamp, but the former receives about three times the latter's amount.

## Effect of light intensity

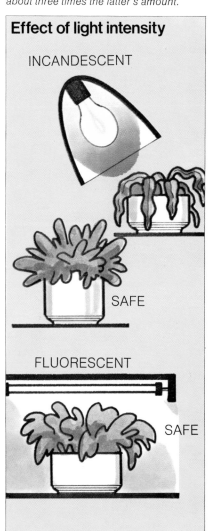

INCANDESCENT

SAFE

FLUORESCENT

SAFE

Incandescent bulbs of enough light intensity for plant growth can also burn a plant that is too close. Radiant heat in the narrow zone surrounding the bulb can reach 100° and more from even a low-wattage lamp. Radiation decreases rapidly, though, and a plant a few inches away is safe.

# Artificial light gardening

Microclimates can be altered with the installation of fluorescent lights which allow you to grow healthy plants in any part of your house. Even attics, basements and dark hallways can be turned into thriving gardens with year-round consistent lighting and controlled climate.

The basic set-up for growing plants under artificial light consists of a standard industrial fluorescent unit with reflector that can be adjusted to stand 12 to 24 inches above the surface on which plants will be placed. Units can be constructed from utilitarian steel shelving and a fluorescent fixture with two or three 40-watt tubes for each 2 by 4 feet growing area. Prefabricated units can be purchased in many designs.

Prof. Fred G. Lechner, agricultural engineer at the NY State College of Agricultural and Life Sciences, Cornell, has recently designed a unit with moving plant trays. The trays travel around a battery of fluorescent tubes installed in a vertical bank at the center of the planter. It takes 18 minutes for a plant to make the orbit around the lights. During the trip the plant receives light from all directions.

The unit is equipped with a bank of 20 lamps, 40 watts each. It may be the only lighting you need for a room. Materials for the frame cost about $200. Plans are available from the Department of Agricultural Engineering, Cornell University. A bulletin explaining four other artificial light units, along with plans for building them, is available for 35 cents from the Mailing Room, Research Park, Ithaca, NY 14850. Ask for Information Bulletin 40, "Cornell Automated Plant Grower."

Fluorescent tubes can be installed over existing shelving or directly in the ceiling to benefit large plants. Such lighting is sometimes unflattering and best employed when the room is not occupied.

There are many kinds of fluorescent tubes available. The time-proved combination of one Cool White with one Warm White is hard to beat. Many gardeners swear by the special agricultural growth tubes. Regardless of the type chosen, they should illuminate the plants 12 to 16 hours every day. Less time does not give good growth; more is of no benefit and may be harmful. Automatic timers

*Fluorescent light gardening can be simple or quite elaborate. Above, a basement is turned into a flourishing garden, with potting table and sprouting area. Below, an expensive, timed light unit especially useful for propagating plants in order to have early spring flower beds or get the jump on spring vegetable planting.*

should be used to give the right growing period daily.

Cool beam incandescent floodlights, illuminated several hours each evening, are beneficial to supplement daylight for a large indoor tree or collection. For plants with little natural light, use the floods 12 to 14 hours out of every 24.

*Above: A fluorescent unit is the indoor gardener's aid in propagation and a mobile cart filled with plants uses incandescent light as an aid in the evening. Below: A pebble tray of water on top of the low temperature radiator adds moisture to the air.*

# Heat, ventilation and humidity

The zone in front of a fireplace, an electric radiant heater, a forced air furnace regulator, or any other dry heat source is a hazardous location. Leaves close to it are soon dried up. Rising hot air from the heater, particularly the strong draft of the fireplace, tends to draw moisture from the entire plant.

Hot water radiators, operating at lower temperatures than dry heat stoves, are safer for nearby plants. Never locate one directly on or above it in the rising hot air column. However, some gardeners report success when the radiator is turned very low, covered with a thick layer of asbestos or marble and topped by a metal tray filled with pebbles and water.

A centrally heated house has fewer microclimates than one warmed less thoroughly by unit heaters. You have a better choice of locations when you control the temperature room by room, or even wall by wall. Keep registers and interior doors closed to help regulate central heating.

Outside heat radiates in to burn plants on hot days. In cold weather, particularly at night, the situation reverses. Heat radiates from the warmer room outdoors through the window pane, creating a cold zone behind the glass. A plant can suffer frost damage in this area, especially if its leaves touch the window and radiate directly outside. A drapery, thermopane, glass, a layer of newspapers, or corrugated cardboard help conserve the heat and protect the plant.

Behind a large expanse of glass, accumulating cold air subsides to the floor and spreads, creating an extensive danger zone during the night. Keep plants away from it and off the floor during chillier weather.

Fresh air circulation is essential to plant health, and room humidity is higher near an outside opening. But direct blasts and drafts draw moisture from foliage, or chill a plant in cold weather. Best locations are as close to the opening as other factors allow, but out of the draft. (In chilly periods, a door without weatherstripping can leak enough cold air to damage a plant.)

Open their top sections only, or install deflectors, to allow draft-free circulation at windows.

Maintaining a humidity high

enough for plant health is always a problem, aggravated in winter by continuous operation of heating systems. Both air and soil dry quickly.

Evaporation of water from a tray beneath the plant is a simple method of humidification. Support the container on a bed of pebbles for drainage and ventilation of the roots.

Spraying the leaves of many plants is another way to increase water vapor in the air. (If the air is cold, however, don't spray. The temperature drop from evaporative cooling may be enough to chill the plant.) Most cactus and plants with fuzzy leaves do not like to be misted.

Water according to both indoor and outdoor conditions. Plants use less water on cool cloudy days than on warm bright ones; less moisture is lost by evaporation in cool rooms than warm ones. Avoid drowning plant roots by providing proper drainage through an opening in the container.

Air conditioning is not harmful to plants if the air circulates. Cold lower layers of stagnant chilly air can accumulate in a tightly closed room. Avoid the cold drafts at outlets.

*Plants need fresh air. Keep them as near an open window as possible but away from drafts. The bottom diagram shows the plant close to fresh air but protected from cold.*

## Cross ventilation draft

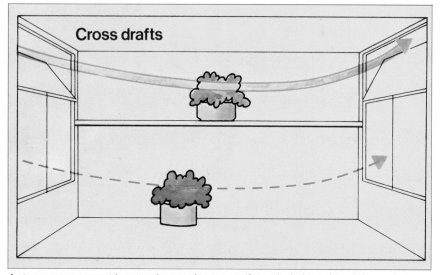

*Cross ventilation creates a strong circulation pattern. A, between two windows, is caught in the path but B is protected.*

### Cross drafts

*A strong cross current is set up by opening top sections of windows, harmful to a plant on the wall but not at floor level. Opening lower sections only would reverse potential damage zones.*

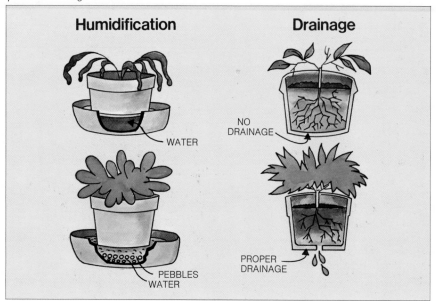

### Humidification    Drainage

WATER

PEBBLES WATER

NO DRAINAGE

PROPER DRAINAGE

*Evaporation of water from a tray beneath the plant is a simple method of humidification. Support the container on a bed of pebbles for drainage and ventilation of the roots. Avoid plant asphyxiation by providing proper drainage for its roots.*

# Microclimates and multiple housing

More and more Americans move to dwellings such as mobile homes, condominiums, apartments, or townhouses.

Mobile homes have become extremely popular and are thoughtfully landscaped, outdoors and indoors, by many owners. In many mobile home parks, the owners of the homes work together with the owner of the park, to develop a community plan. Individual indoor gardening conditions, except for what sometimes may be less space and the limited choice of solar exposures, are otherwise similar to any conventional urban or suburban home. And, usually, unit heaters instead of central heating systems simplify temperature control.

The solid common walls in most multiple housing units severely restrict the amount of available light and solar exposure. A unit in a large apartment block may have only one outside wall, and that on a shady north side. The range of plants able to grow under such conditions is narrow. Check the listing on page 54 under "Plants for shaded locations." Also consider supplementary fluorescent tubes. Hanging baskets or shelves across the windows add extra dimensions for gardening.

Central heating makes humidity and temperature control a difficult problem. Gardening may be limited to a small confined climate, as an enclosed bay window or terrarium. Use portable humidifiers to add moisture to the air. Consider installing prefab window greenhouse units for added growing space.

When hampered by unfavorable interior conditions, an apartment gardener uses his balconies or terrace as much as possible in search of favorable plant zones. Orientation of the building determines whether exposure and wind control is excellent or poor. Unless a small balcony is enclosed as a plant room, he must take the same precautions as an outdoor gardener against heat and cold.

The tendency toward towering apartment buildings creates a new set of high-rise microclimates.

Top floors are cooler, due to height and remoteness from heat-radiating streets and lower structures. Winds, less obstructed by surface structures, blow stronger and more freely. A low fog may shroud ground floors while upper ones are sunny. Street fumes and dust are more prevalent at lower levels. An adjacent building may block solar exposures to certain heights.

Metropolitan gardening is possible and pleasurable, but its conditions are much more complicated, restrictive and challenging than those of suburban areas.

*Right: A garden of herbs, vegetables and flowers grown in packing crates fill a terrace for the city gardener. Below: The beginnings of a bean crop against the cityscape in a highrise apartment. Gardening in such an urban environment brings the city dweller in touch with the earth.*

# Confined climates

Confined climates are one of a gardener's ways of outwitting the weather. Through their use, flowers and fruits grow where nature never intended. The growing period can be stretched to a year-round length, no matter what the location or season.

These enclosures range from small protected spaces, modifying an existing climate for the benefit of a seedling, to elaborate structures where climate is completely controlled and any type of growing conditions may be reproduced.

Experienced gardeners look upon one or more of them as indispensable tools to all-year plant culture.

Air space can be confined by small containers in many little ways to create more favorable growing conditions or stretch the season.

Indoors, an enclosed bay window solves humidity problems as does a small greenhouse. Exterior shading for hot sun, a heater in frosty weather, and ventilation must be considered.

If ventilated, a terrarium supports tiny plants. An inverted drinking glass would even suffice for some.

A plastic bag slipped over a house plant while you're away a few days conserves moisture till you return. Cut holes for ventilation.

Outdoors, confined climates work on the coldframe principle, admitting insolation and lessening outgoing radiation.

A hotcap is a common example, giving you a two to four week head start on the normal growing season.

Scraps of glass, and plastic film-covered frames in many conformations are quick, simple variations of the coldframe.

◊

*A young lady gardens in a geodesic model from Redwood Domes. Below are two versions of the classic shape by Lord and Burnham.*

*Small confined, controlled climates include (clockwise, beginning upper left) the "solar window" from Aladdin Industries; miniature conservatory-type terrarium; a plant bagged to hold moisture while gardener is away; an environmental case by Lord and Burnham and a mobile window conservatory by Casaplanta.*

## Small confined climates

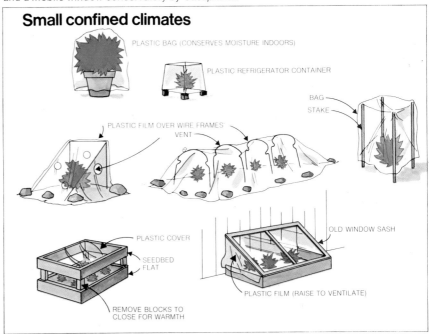

PLASTIC BAG (CONSERVES MOISTURE INDOORS)

PLASTIC REFRIGERATOR CONTAINER

BAG
STAKE

PLASTIC FILM OVER WIRE FRAMES
VENT

PLASTIC COVER

SEEDBED
FLAT

OLD WINDOW SASH

PLASTIC FILM (RAISE TO VENTILATE)

REMOVE BLOCKS TO
CLOSE FOR WARMTH

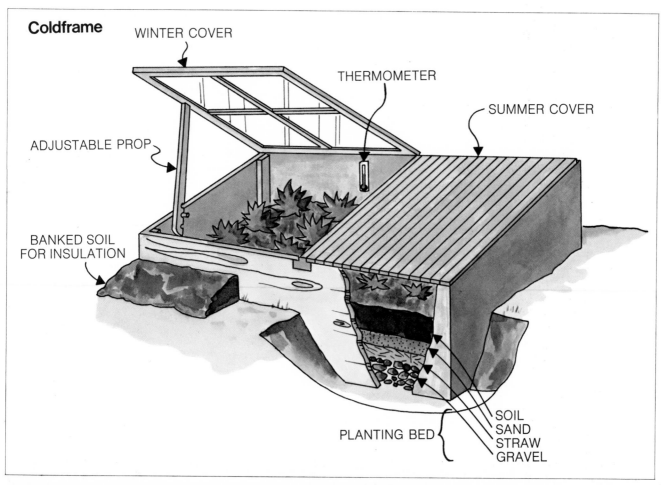

**Coldframe**

WINTER COVER

THERMOMETER

SUMMER COVER

ADJUSTABLE PROP

BANKED SOIL
FOR INSULATION

PLANTING BED

SOIL
SAND
STRAW
GRAVEL

*This coldframe on legs allows storage below. Addition of heating cable converts it to hotbed.*

# Coldframes and hotbeds

A coldframe is a small greenhouse in principle. Structurally it is a bottomless, glass-covered box, heated only by the sun for the propagation, growing, and protection of plants.

The wooden box is airtight construction, treated with wood preservative, painted, and sunk into the ground. Its hinged transparent window is stock coldframe sash (available from greenhouse supply firms), or an old window or glass door. (You can also build a polyethylene-film-covered frame.) Fill the planting bed with layers of gravel, straw, sand, and soil.

Orient the coldframe to the south sun, on a well drained site. A fence or wall on the north side is excellent wind protection and reflects additional light and heat into the box. White or silver paint on inside walls also reflect more light to the plants. Notch transverse mullions to facilitate water runoff.

Equip the coldframe with a thermometer. When it reads above the optimum growing level, open the sash to permit air circulation to reduce it. Close it again when temperatures start to drop, to conserve radiation absorbed by the soil.

In cooler weather, insulate the outer sides of the box with banked soil or sawdust. Cover the top with sacks stuffed with straw or excelsior, wood planks, or other insulation during cold nights or chilly overcast days.

During hot weather, solar radiation to the coldframe is reduced by shading devices similar to those of the greenhouse. A mist spray can humidify and cool the air.

In milder climates a coldframe provides frost protection and temperatures that keep plants growing through the winter.

It will do the same in cold winter areas if a heating system is added, converting it to a hotbed.

## Soil heating cable installation

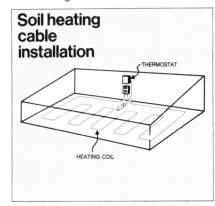

The cable is laid 6 or 7 inches deep in the soil or sand of the plant bed, following a fret pattern that brings no strand of the wire less than 6 inches from another. A thermostat inside the box regulates its operation.

In earlier times a layer of fresh horse manure generated the heat, but today the usual source is an electric soil-heating cable.

(Incandescent lamp bulbs under the glass can also warm the box, though not as well as the cable.)

Portable coldframes and hotbeds are available as commercial products.

# Sun-heated pit greenhouses

The pit greenhouse could be described as a coldframe with headroom. Heated entirely by insolation, it does not require as much constant attention as the conventional type.

Its structure is glass on one side, facing south at a 45-degree angle, and an insulated roof on the other.

Below it, a pit at least 4 feet deep is lined with a concrete or concrete-block wall which also supports the superstructure.

A drainage layer extends about a foot deeper. Fist-sized stones at the bottom are graduated to a crushed stone walking surface.

Skylights in the north roof and openings at the end provide for ventilation and heat reduction. The opening at the more sheltered end is the entrance, somewhat cramped but passable.

Though the tropic varieties of a conventional greenhouse cannot be grown within it, the pit keeps most

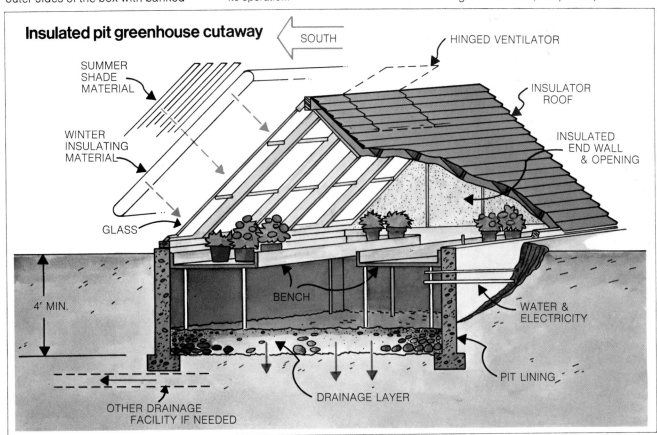

**Insulated pit greenhouse cutaway**

SOUTH

SUMMER SHADE MATERIAL

WINTER INSULATING MATERIAL

GLASS

4' MIN.

OTHER DRAINAGE FACILITY IF NEEDED

BENCH

DRAINAGE LAYER

HINGED VENTILATOR

INSULATOR ROOF

INSULATED END WALL & OPENING

WATER & ELECTRICITY

PIT LINING

*Sunken pit greenhouses rely on energy from the sun for heat. Even in cold winter climates additional heating may not be necessary, but can be added to grow plants that enjoy warmth. Construction and upkeep costs are minimal.*

temperate zone plants safe and blooming through the winter.

The large volume of sun-heated confined air, and radiation from the ground, have held inside temperatures above freezing levels during 18-degrees-below nights.

Thick insulating pads help retain the heat at night or on cold cloudy days.

If current is available, a small electric heater quickly warms the interior in emergencies or provides supplementary light, though such additions dilute the pure form of the pit.

Designed primarily for winter gardening, this greenhouse may be used in summer as well when shading devices are provided.

## Variations of pit greenhouse

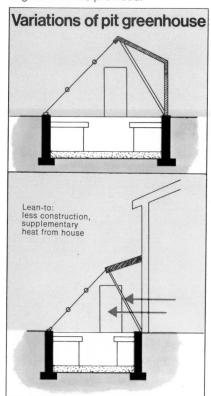

Lean-to:
less construction,
supplementary
heat from house

*Here are two variations of the standard A design to provide more headroom or as a lean-to.*

*Sturdi-built's unusual "Sun flare" model is prefabricated of redwood in three sizes. The circular design is convenient for container gardening and efficient to heat.*

*A window greenhouse, top left, requires little space. Model shown is by J. A. Nearing Co. Interior greenhouse photos emphasize pleasures of controlled climate gardening. The lean-to construction (bottom) by National adds extra room as well as year-round garden.*

# Greenhouses

A greenhouse is the most sophisticated type of confined climate. Properly equipped and managed, it assures virtually complete weather control. Within it, you can grow exotic plants from the humid tropics, out-of-season fruits and vegetables, and flowers of any species.

The typical home greenhouse is a light framework of wood or metal, sheathed with clear glass above the level of the plant benches. It may be home-made or prefabricated, ranging in price from $100 to thousands.

Essential features are adjustable ventilators at its ridge and base for air circulation; thermostat, space heater and fan; humidistat and humidifiers to regulate air moisture; and an electrical circuit.

It depends upon the sun as its primary heat source, supplemented at night or in cold weather by the heater.

Operating principles are simple enough. If the temperature within is too high, open the ventilators or use an extractor fan to reduce it.

If too low, bring it to the proper level with the heater. When air is dry, add moisture with the mist from the humidifiers, (which also provide evaporative cooling).

Overhead fluorescent lights can supplement the natural supply during overcast weather and short winter days.

*A relatively inexpensive fiberglass prefab unit at the top is distributed by McGregor. The A-line freestanding greenhouse from Sturdi-built is prefabricated of redwood. Lath extensions provide shading and protection for glass walls.*

## Greenhouse equipment

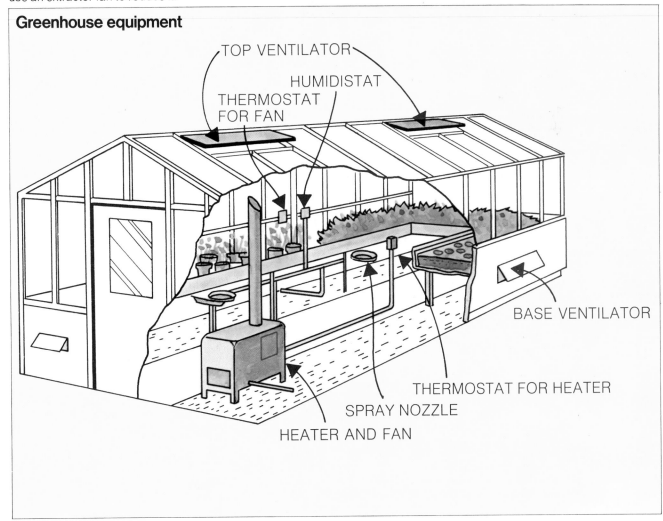

TOP VENTILATOR

HUMIDISTAT

THERMOSTAT FOR FAN

BASE VENTILATOR

THERMOSTAT FOR HEATER

SPRAY NOZZLE

HEATER AND FAN

Three different available freestanding prefabricated models. Top: 'Crystalaire' by Peter Reimuller; Middle: Geodesic dome designed by Redwood Domes; Bottom: Traditional styling manufactured by Ickes-Braun Glasshouses.

Greenhouse management is an almost continual process, particularly in periods of bad weather. A sharp temperature drop in the night can wipe out valuable plants unless you're on hand to prevent it.

Controls may be operated manually if you're around the house most

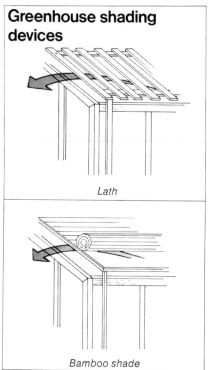

**Greenhouse shading devices**

*Lath*

*Bamboo shade*

*Additional exterior controls are necessary during summer months to temper the insolation. Lath strips, muslin, plastic, or other shade devices should be suspended above the roof to permit air circulation. A roller-blind type is adjustable to the season. Whitewash or greenhouse paint is often used for shading. It screens in summer, weather erodes gradually to admit needed winter sun.*

of the day. However, an automatic system can activate all of them when required, giving you more peace of mind and a sounder sleep.

A soil heating cable can be installed in the propagating bed for speedy germination.

A home greenhouse correspondence course is offered by Pennsylvania State University. Write to: Correspondence Courses in Agriculture, 202 Agricultural Education Building, The Pennsylvania State University, University Park, PA 16802.

For additional information and/or catalogues, contact greenhouse distributors.

# Greenhouse sources

**(1) Agricultural Engineering Dept.**
Pennsylvania State University
University Park, PA 16802
*Plans for many types of greenhouses; also information on construction and environmental control.*

**(2) Aladdin Industries**
P.O. Box 10666
Nashville, TN 37201
*Indoor greenhouse cases and window units.*

**(3) Aluminum Greenhouses, Inc.**
14615 Lorain Avenue
Cleveland, OH 44111
*Freestanding and lean-to lightweight models.*

**(4) American Leisure Industries**
Box 63
Deep River, CT 06417
*Freestanding greenhouses.*

**(5) Casa-planta**
9489 Dayton Way
Beverly Hills, CA 90210
*Inexpensive modular, vinyl-covered.*

**(6) Feather Hill Industries**
Box 41
Zenda, WI 53195
*Unusual bubble-type window units.*

**(7) Geodesic Domes**
RR 1, Bloomington, IL 61701

**(8) Gothic Arch Greenhouses**
Box 1564
Mobile, AL 36601
*Freestanding prefabs.*

**(9) Greenhouse Specialties Company**
9849 Kimker Lane
St. Louis, MO 63127
*Plans and fiberglass samples.*

**(10) Hansen Weather-Port**
313 North Taylor
Gunnison, CO 81230
*Portable units.*

**(11) Ickes-Braun Glasshouses**
P. O. Box 147
Deerfield, IL 60015
*Complete supplies for building your own design.*

**(12) Lord and Burnham**
Irvington, NY 10533
*All sizes, window units to large freestanding models.*

**(13) Maco Home Greenhouses**
Box 109
Scio, OR 97374
*Inexpensive greenhouses.*

**(14) A. S. Margulies Company**
34 Porter Road
Chelmsford, MA 01824
*Miniature units: plastic covered.*

**(15) McGregor Greenhouses**
Box 36
Santa Cruz, CA 95063
*Fiberglass prefabs.*

**(16) Mid America Greenhouse Company**
10907 Manchester
St. Louis, MO 63122

**(17) National Greenhouse Company**
P. O. Box 100
Pana, IL 62557
*Freestanding models, many sizes.*

**(18) J. A. Nearing Company**
10788 Tucker Street
Beltsville, MD 20705
*Aluminum greenhouses; window units to large commercial sizes.*

**(19) Portabilt**
Box 12212
Tucson, AZ 85711
*Vinyl-covered models.*

**(20) Redfern Greenhouses**
55 Mount Hermon Road
Scotts Valley, CA 95060
*Prefab lean-to and freestanding.*

**(21) Redwood Domes**
P. O. Box 666
Aptos, CA 95003
*Geodesic dome greenhouses.*

**(22) Peter Reimuller**
Box 2666
Santa Cruz, CA 95060
*Inexpensive vinyl-covered models.*

**(23) Sturdi-Built Manufacturing Co.**
11304 S.W. Boones Ferry Road
Portland, OR 97219
*Prefab home units.*

**(24) Texas Greenhouse Company**
2717 St. Louis Avenue
Fort Worth, TX 76110
*Prefab aluminum and redwood units.*

**(25) Turner Greenhouses**
Box 1260
Goldsboro, NC 27530
*Inexpensive greenhouses.*

**(26) University of Illinois**
College of Agriculture
Cooperative Extension Service
Urbana-Champaign, IL 61801
*Plans for simple greenhouse by J. W. Courter and J. O. Curtis.*

**(27) Verandel Company**
Box 1568
Worcest, MA 01611
*Inexpensive lean-to greenhouses.*

*Redfern offers a unit constructed of redwood frame with glass walls and fiberglass roofing in several sizes.*

# Under-standing weather

Everyone talks weather. We are kept weather conscious through continuing reports of up-to-the-minute weather happenings and forecasts via television, radio and newspapers. Do you really understand the meaning of all this weather talk?

Here we hope to clarify some of the physical principles which relate to your own daily weather changes. Also included in our alphabetical listing is basic terminology used by the weather experts, which should become part of the vocabulary of the weather-wise gardener.

**Air mass paths.** On weather charts, masses are labeled "T" if tropical in source, and "P" if their origin is polar. If formed over land, they are designated "c" (continental), or "m" (maritime) if they form above an ocean. A third designation may be added to indicate whether the air is colder (k) or warmer (w) than surface over which it passes.

Continental polar air moving over ground warmer than itself, therefore, is marked "cPk."

A cP air mass is cold and dry, and causes rain over the United States when it picks up moisture over the Great Lakes or meets differing air masses. Moisture is present in "mP air," and the mass can warm up over a longer ocean path. A mass of mT air is always humid and warm at its source, and creates much of our precipitation as it meets colder masses.

Study of the typical air mass paths across the country, their continental and maritime characteristics, and their temperatures help us to understand their part in shaping our macroclimates.

The masses tend to follow certain seasonal paths, retaining their original temperature and moisture conditions.

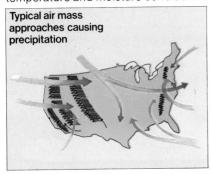

Typical air mass approaches causing precipitation

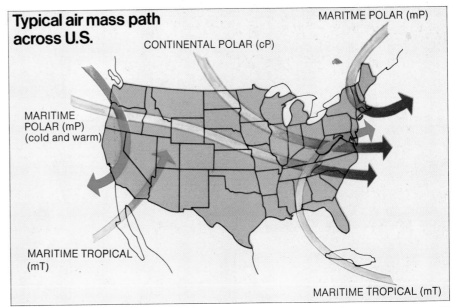

## Typical air mass path across U.S.

MARITME POLAR (mP)

CONTINENTAL POLAR (cP)

MARITIME POLAR (mP) (cold and warm)

MARITIME TROPICAL (mT)

MARITIME TROPICAL (mT)

But the tracks vary, and the characteristics are modified by the relatively warmer or cooler surfaces below them.

If warmer than the surface below, the mass becomes stable as its lower layers are cooled and compacted. When the situation is reversed, the heated lower air struggles upward through the cold above, often producing gusty winds, clouds, showers and other disturbances.

**Atmospheric circulation, primary.** The equator, more perpendicular to

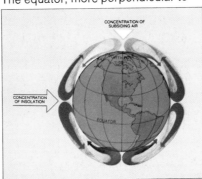

the radiation, absorbs more heat than the polar regions. The light hot air of the tropics rises into the atmosphere, is displaced by cool air flowing in from the poles. The circulation thus set up becomes our major weather generator.

If the earth stood still, we would have perpetual north-south winds from this massive air movement, or south-north if we lived in the southern hemisphere.

**Anemometer.** Any instrument for measuring the speed of the wind.

**Atmospheric circulation, secondary.** Directions are deflected by the rotation of the globe as the air masses move between the equator and the poles to create our prevailing wind patterns.

**Atmospheric filtering (concentration of insolation).** The unequal heating of the earth's surface stirs the atmos-

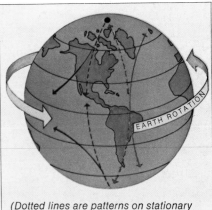

*(Dotted lines are patterns on stationary globe). Blue is subsiding air, red is rising air.*

phere like a giant spoon. The major cause of this temperature differential is the angle at which the solar rays strike the surface of the planet.

When a ray's angle of contact is more perpendicular to the surface, its effect is concentrated in a smaller area. As the angle decreases, a greater amount of surface is covered. The total energy output is the same in either case; it's just more widely distributed.

Acting as a filter to solar radiation, the atmosphere also plays its part in the general heat distribution. A ray from a 90-degree angle has less distance to travel through the atmospheric belt than one approaching from a 45-degree angle. The effectiveness of the latter is reduced by the additional elongation.

So we can see how the difference in the directness of the insolation causes the unequal heating of the major areas of the globe, creating the climatic extremes of the equatorial and polar zones which set the whole circulation pattern of the world's weather in motion.

## Climatic variations

*I. Macroclimate.* General weather pattern of a large region. The Pacific Northwest, the Rocky Mountains, the Great Plains, or the Gulf Coast all have their own climate identities, governed by predictable movements of air masses.

The physical appearance and plant growth of a region indicate its place in the categories of the United States, which may be humid (forest), sub-

## Climate map by vegetation

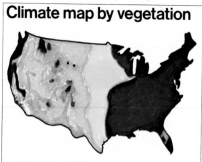

humid (grassland), semiarid (steppe), or arid (desert).

## United States Macroclimates

1 Long cold winter, hot summer, wide temperature range; high humidity and precipitation; northwest winter storms, scant summer wind. Look for: fall, winter, and spring sunshine; protection from storms but good secondary circulation against humidity; dry, well-drained ground.

2 Cool winter with some cold snaps; long, hot, oppressive summer; few topographic climatic differences; humid with moderate rainfall. Look for: sun protection, good air circulation.

3 Hot glaring summer, short mild winter, even temperature; humid, tropic. Look for: good air circulation, well-drained sites; protection against low western and eastern sun.

4 Cold winters, hot summers, wide temperature range; humid. Look for: storm protection, well-drained sites.

5 Cold winter, hot summer, wide temperature variation with extreme changes; low humidity, semi-arid. Look for: winter sunshine, year-round wind protection.

6 Very cold winter, warm summer; great climatic variety; low humidity and rainfall. Look for: sunshine, protection from prevailing and secondary winds.

7 Very hot summer, mild winter; very dry atmosphere; strong glaring sun. Look for: sun control, year-round wind protection.

8 Cool summer, mild winter; high humidity and precipitation, damp ground. Look for: protection against westerly winds, well-drained site.

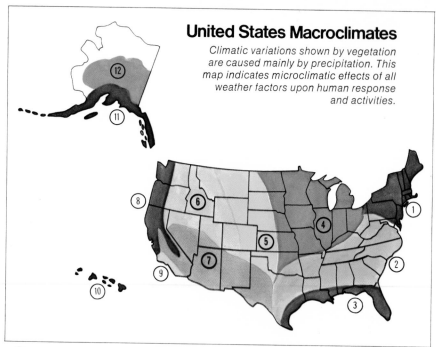

# United States Macroclimates

*Climatic variations shown by vegetation are caused mainly by precipitation. This map indicates microclimatic effects of all weather factors upon human response and activities.*

9 Cool summer, mild winter; humid with low rainfall. Look for: south and west sun protection, protection against prevailing wind.

10 Warm summer, mild winter; humid, light to heavy precipitation; sharp changes in rainfall patterns. Look for: air circulation in windless exposures, well-drained sites in rainy areas.

11 Cool summers, relatively mild winters. Rainy, humid. Year-round climate moderated by warm Alaska current.

12 Very cold winters. Mild summers. Occasional hot spell up to 100° Short, intensive growing season. Long daylight hours.

*II. Mesoclimate.* Intermediate variations in the big general weather of an entire region. Weather in San Francisco is quite different than that of Los Angeles, but both are mesoclimates within the same macroclimate. The simplest answer to the

variations lies in the degree of exposure to the big weathermaking factors. One area may be warmer than another because it receives more solar radiation, because of its latitudinal position, the slope of the ground, or possibly because cloudier conditions screen out more insolation. Another location may be rainier than another because of a closer proximity to a storm track, or because it is less "shadowed" by a terrain feature.

The rugged topography of the west, with high peaks adjacent to low-lying valleys, rolling hills and lofty plateaus, visually illustrates the fact that the more irregular the terrain the more varied its climates will be.

Moderating effects of large bodies of water create more mesoclimates, again more pronounced when combined with terrain features. A sea coast may be shrouded in cooling fog while

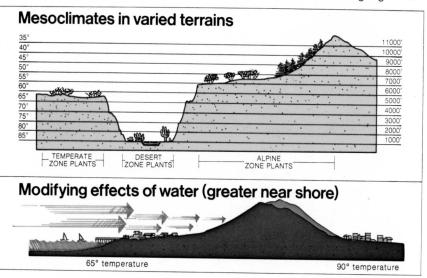

## Mesoclimates in varied terrains

| TEMPERATE ZONE PLANTS | DESERT ZONE PLANTS | ALPINE ZONE PLANTS |

## Modifying effects of water (greater near shore)

65° temperature          90° temperature

a valley a few miles inland, shut off from the marine airflow by mountains, swelters in a temperature 30 degrees higher.

*III. Microclimate.* Little intimate weathers changing from street to street through the city, from one side to another of a hilltop, and virtually foot by foot about the garden or in the house.

## Cloud types

*1. Alto-cumulus.* High, fleecy clouds in round, white or grayish, partly shaded masses.

*2. Alto-stratus.* Fibrous gray or bluish sheet, usually thick enough to cast a shadow.

*3. Cirro-cumulus.* High, small white, fleecy clouds in groups or rows (also called mackerel sky).

*4. Cirro-stratus.* High, delicate, milky sheet, resembling a tangled web.

*5. Cirrus.* Wispy, whitish, high clouds formed from ice crystals. No precipitation, may be a sign of approaching warm front.

*6. Cumulo-cirrus.* Small cumulus cloud that is white and filmy like a cirrus.

*7. Cumulo-nimbus.* Thick, towering thunderheads, second greatest rainmaker.

*8. Cumulo-stratus.* Cumulus cloud with horizontal base like a stratus.

*9. Cumulus.* Billowy white fair weather clouds.

*10. Nimbo-stratus.* Low, dark, ragged cloud layer responsible for most of our precipitation.

*11. Stratus.* Low uniform layer, resembling fog, but not resting on the ground. May produce a drizzle.

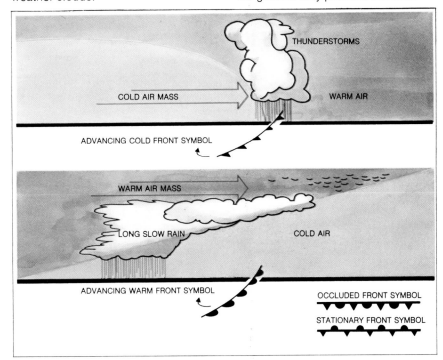

*12. Strato-cumulus.* Long parallel, dark rolls pushed together, or soft gray broken masses.

**Dew point.** The temperature to which the air must be cooled for it to reach saturation; the temperature at which dew begins to form.

**Foot-candle.** A unit for measuring illumination. One foot-candle is equal to the amount of direct light thrown by one international candle on a square foot of surface every part of which is one foot away.

**Fronts (warm and cold).** Air masses refuse to mix unless their temperature and moisture content are very similar. A boundary between them, the weather "front," forms at the line of collision between a warm and a cold air mass.

A "cold front" develops when an advancing cold air mass meets a warm one. The denser air of its leading edge burrows below the lighter air of the latter, wedging it aloft to produce clouds, gusty winds, and thunderstorms. If it is moving rapidly the disturbance can be a violent "squall line" as the warm air is abruptly raised, but its effects pass quickly.

A slow-moving cold front lifts the warm air more gradually; storms may be mild or non-existent. Its conditions are more widespread and longer lasting, however.

*Cirrus.* Good weather if winds from W NW to N. Precipitation likely if winds steady NE E to S.

*Cirrocumulus.* If seen on early summer morning and winds NE to S, evening rain likely.

*Altostratus.* Fibrous appearing cloud screens sun. Precipitation in 12 to 24 hours if NE to S winds.

*Stratus.* May bring heavy precipitation if winds NE to S. Other winds bring overcast or drizzle.

*Cumulus.* Fair weather clouds, if no vertical development extending upwards.

*Cumulonimbus.* Thunderheads likely to bring precipitation soon if winds from SW W to N.

A "warm front" forms as an advancing warm air mass slides up and over the retreating cold air mass. The action is usually slower than that of a cold front, storms develop gradually but are more widespread and long lasting. Surface winds are normally mild, but turbulence and thunderstorms can occur aloft.

An "occluded front" develops as a cold mass overtakes a warm one on the same course, sliding under it to lift the whole warm mass above the surface. Fronts of this type can appear regularly across the United States, due to prevailing influence of the westerlies on weather and generally faster movement of the cold air masses.

When neither mass prevails a "stationary front" forms. Conditions are usually similar to those of the warm front, as long as it is stabilized. If it does move, the characteristics of the mass exerting the influence are adopted.

The movements, sizes, and strong

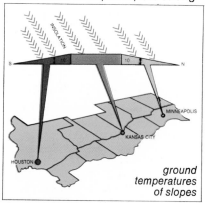

ground temperatures of slopes

characteristics of the different fronts are the most meaningful predictors of oncoming weather. The symbols defining the fronts on the meteorologists' charts mark the zones of the most intense activity.

## Ground temperature of slopes.
On smaller and more localized scales, slopes can duplicate some of the conditions causing the torrid temperatures of the equatorial zones and the frigid weathers of the polar regions.

The southward tilt of the ground in a temperate climate places the surface in a more perpendicular relationship to incoming radiation; a slant to the north disperses it over a wider area. Thusly, a normal flat-ground climate is directed toward more tropic or more alpine conditions.

In a western canyon, pines, oaks, and other temperate zone trees may grow on the north slope, while its south exposure may have only a covering of grass or some sparse desert vegetation. Though air temperatures are similar, the wide

## Air action and ground temperatures on slopes

variation in ground temperatures regulate the kind and the amount of life on the opposite sides. The north slopes also retain their moisture longer.

**Heat and moisture changes.** The capacity of air to hold water vapor decreases as its temperatures lessen. As it rises, it cools below its saturation point and the moisture condenses to form clouds. If the moisture content is high enough, it produces rain.

Forced upward by a mountain range, the moisture is literally wrung out of an air mass.

Descending the opposite slope, the air is warmed again and retains the water vapor still left within it.

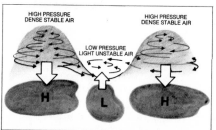

## High and low pressure systems.
Circulation of the great masses of unequally heated air creates whirling cells at different atmospheric pressures. High pressure develops where air cools, compresses, and sinks. Major low-pressure areas are formed in the troughs between highs.

Winds blow clockwise around a high; counterclockwise from a low. The former generally indicates fair weather, while the latter brings storms.

Sizes and positions of the major pressure areas vary seasonally. They, and the general air circulation patterns, determine the distribution of moisture throughout the world.

## High and low seasonal positions.
The seasonal positions of the persistent high and low pressure areas are important to climatic regulation. The highs form mostly over the oceans in the northern hemisphere, particularly when the land is warm in the summer, and are greater in size than the lows.

A high can act as a barrier against

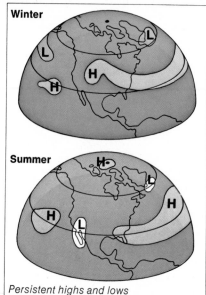

*Persistent highs and lows*

the stormy weather spawned by a pressure area. The Pacific High, for instance, shields Southern California during the warmer parts of the year from the rains which drench Western Washington.

In addition to the major pressure areas, numbers of lesser highs and lows form more or less regularly over land and sea to vary weather patterns.

**Hurricane.** A violent cyclonic storm with winds moving at 73 or more miles per hour, originating in the tropics, especially the West Indies region. Winds of hurricane force sometimes occur in the absence of a hurricane system.

**Hydrologic cycle.** The water vapor that forms clouds and precipitation begins for the most part as evaporation from the soil, rivers, lakes and the oceans. Also, vegetation gives off moisture (transpiration). Water vapor is transported through the air, forming clouds, then condensing into some form of precipitation. On reaching the earth the water flows in rivulets and streams to the rivers, or filters into the ground to replenish the ground water supply that also feeds the rivers. Thus, most of the water that was evaporated from the ocean eventually finds its way back to the ocean.

**Hygrometer.** Any instrument for measuring the water-vapor content of the atmosphere.

**Insolation.** Incoming solar energy. Its intensity is regulated by the angle at which the sun's rays strike the earth's surface, by atmospheric conditions, ground textures, vegetation or structure, and numerous other natural or artificial controls. Variations in the amount of radiation received trigger the reactions shaping our climatic differences. See: solar energy.

**Insolation absorption (storing solar energy).** We can use the absorptive qualities of different surfaces to increase their heat storage capacity in chillier climates, or to lessen it in warmer ones.

Water is by far the best heat storage reservoir we have. The ocean absorbs 95% of the insolation it receives, reflecting little back into the atmosphere. It is a very slow radiator, and its day and night temperatures are more constant than those of faster-radiating land surfaces.

These qualities are sometimes used for protection during short frost periods, flooding the ground to gain heat from the water and slow outgoing radiation. (The process must be used cautiously, however. Evaporative cooling from sprinkled leaves on damp ground can chill a surface as well.)

The density of granite, and other stone and masonry, holds their absorption capabilities at higher levels ranging from about 50% to 70%.

Average soil absorbs and stores about 30% of the insolation. When cultivated, however, the figure drops to about 20%, as the air spaces created are poor conductors of heat. The capacity of light soil is less than that of dark soil, as light colors reflect more and absorb less than dark ones. The capacities of sand and peat are greater when damp, with their air spaces filled with water.

Grass and leaf litter, because of their many air spaces, are at the bottom end of the scale with only 5% storage capacity. Snow is very poor, because of its air content and highly reflective qualities.

By absorbing more insolation during the day, a surface slows down its heat loss at night. This is illustrated on some chilly mornings by frost patches on the grass but not on adjacent soil.

Ground temperatures can be altered through the use of materials with different absorptive properties.

Gardeners, commercial growers, and farmers modify ground conditions with mulches. Older methods of mulching utilized the absorptive qualities of stones to conduct additional heat to the soil, spreading them around the base of the plant. The principle is still valid, and is still seen in some gardens and orchards.

Bricks have the same effect, and can be used in a decorative manner.

Stones, still seen in small European vineyards, are spread around the base of a plant to conduct more heat to the soil. Bricks have the same effect, and can be used in a decorative manner.

To moderate the heat, the air spaces in a layer of straw, grass clippings, or leaf litter are an insulating blanket reducing the radiation reaching the ground below them. By the same principle, loose mulches are frost hazards in winter.

Modern farmers turn to plastic film for mulching, covering acres of ground for more favorable soil temperatures, faster seed germination, and better fruit and vegetable quality. The process also controls weed and conserves water. On a smaller scale, home gardeners can use plastic sheets to the same advantage. (See "Mulches," pp. 6-25.)

**Insolation and radiation.** After absorption, insolation is given back to the atmosphere as radiation.

Radiating properties of different materials, when the surfaces are extensive, have a pronounced effect on air temperatures. A rocky canyon can become insufferably hot from the intensity of the radiation projected by the terrain. On the other hand, they can amplify feeble heat rays for pleasant sunpockets in colder sections.

The radiation from the pavements and masonry structures is great enough to give the city its own mesoclimate. The great degree of accumulated heat takes longer to radiate at night, and is further retarded by dust, smog, and other atmospheric debris. Its average temperature is several degrees warmer than the countryside, when radiating surfaces are fewer and heat escapes more rapidly into clearer night air.

**Isobars.** Lines or weather charts connecting points of equal pressure.

**Jetstream.** A stream of very strong wind moving around either of the earth's poles, usually from west to east at altitudes between 10,000 and 50,000 feet. See: Wind.

**Meteorology.** The science dealing with the atmosphere and its phenomena, including weather and climate.

**Moisture distribution.** The elements distribute our rainfall rather haphazardly about the United States. Some areas live under skies which seem perpetually soggy and where fence posts sprout mossy caps; precipitation is rare enough to be a climatic accident in others.

The Pacific coast receives most of its rainfall during the winter periods from frontal storms, from the humid North to semi-arid Southern California. The south coast may not have measurable rainfall from early spring until late fall.

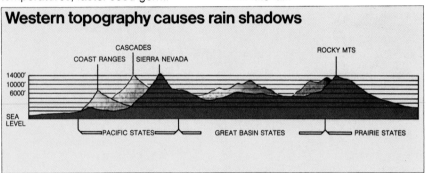

**Western topography causes rain shadows**

Rain shadows from the terrain eliminate the rains from all but the strong storms to limit their spread eastward. Most of the inland west depends on summer thundershowers for its moisture, from the maritime air masses from the Gulf of Mexico or, to a lesser degree, the Gulf of California.

The shadow effect is very pronounced within the Hawaiian rainfall cycle. One side of an island is lush and green, the other arid and bare.

The grasslands of the midwest grain belt depend mostly upon thunderstorms from moisture-charged Gulf of Mexico air for precipitation, concentrated more heavily in summer.

East of the Mississippi, the interactions between the continental and the maritime air masses are more constant, and rain averages more evenly through the year.

Few regions are fortunate enough to receive just the right amount of moisture at the right time by natural means. It's often a matter of too little or too much. Southwestern farmers usually have to irrigate their fields throughout the year, while Florida citrus growers drain surplus ground water from orchards by deep ditches.

**Nephoscope.** An instrument for determining the altitude of clouds and the velocity and direction of their motion.

**Ocean currents.** The giant permanent currents circulating clockwise in the northern hemisphere form bands which can differ as much as 30 degrees from their adjacent surfaces. These have significant effects on continental climate when they closely parallel the coastlines.

The warm Gulf Stream is the dominant current of the Atlantic Coast, tempering its winter weather as far

## Why the ocean is moderating effect on temperature

LARGE % OF INSOLATION STORED

SMALL % RADIATED

SMALL % OF INSOLATION STORED

LARGE % RADIATED

## Major ocean currents

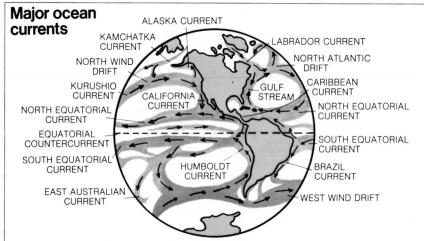

ALASKA CURRENT
KAMCHATKA CURRENT
NORTH WIND DRIFT
KURUSHIO CURRENT
CALIFORNIA CURRENT
NORTH EQUATORIAL CURRENT
EQUATORIAL COUNTERCURRENT
SOUTH EQUATORIAL CURRENT
EAST AUSTRALIAN CURRENT
LABRADOR CURRENT
NORTH ATLANTIC DRIFT
CARIBBEAN CURRENT
GULF STREAM
NORTH EQUATORIAL CURRENT
SOUTH EQUATORIAL CURRENT
HUMBOLDT CURRENT
BRAZIL CURRENT
WEST WIND DRIFT

north as Cape Hatteras. Above this point, the cold waters of the Labrador Current wedge themselves between it and the coastline, forming the so-called "cold wall," contributing to the severity of New England winters and moderating summer heat.

The warm Gulf Stream continues eastward as the North Atlantic Drift, and spreads its benefits as far as northwestern Europe.

The major Pacific current rotates in the same manner, but temperature

characteristics change. The warm Kuroshio (Japan) Current crosses the ocean as the North Pacific Drift. A secondary arm, the Alaska Current, splits off to follow a course along the southern coastline of our largest state and soften its northerly climate.

The mainstream, mixed with frostier waters by now, flows southward as the cool California Current beside the states below the Canadian border.

Damp fogs from the interactions of the differing water, air and land temperatures edge its course in the summer. Chilly water temperatures discourage all but the hardiest swimmers and most of its sun bathers move a few miles inland to deepen a tan. As much as ten inches of annual fog-drip, apart from the plentiful rainfall, have been measured beneath the redwoods of northern California forests during a season.

A strange phenomenon, peculiar to the northern California coast (and Morocco in the northern hemisphere) contributes to the abundant fog. By a natural reaction of water to air movement, the prevailing northwest wind forces water offshore. As the coast acts as a barrier, replacement can come only from the deeper layers of the ocean. The process is termed "upwelling." The rising water is colder and richer in nutrients than that which it replaces. Discouraging to swimmers, it's a productive boon to fishermen.

**Ocean effect on temperature.** The oceans' more even temperatures are carried by air masses overland, moderating extremes of heat and cold. The ocean absorbs and stores virtually all the solar energy reaching it, and re-radiates back only a small percentage. The average difference between surface temperature, winter and summer, is only about 18 degrees. The diurnal variation is less than one degree.

Contrast this to the many extremes of temperature on land surfaces where a small percentage of solar energy is stored and most radiated back. Thus the more even ocean temperatures carried over land act as a gigantic air-conditioning system.

**Precipitation.** Products of condensation in the atmosphere may take many forms.

*Fog* is merely a low lying cloud. When in contact with objects whose surface is at freezing temperatures it leaves an icy deposit called rime.

*Frost* occurs when water vapor (dew)

## Currents affecting U.S. (dark areas cold, light areas warm).

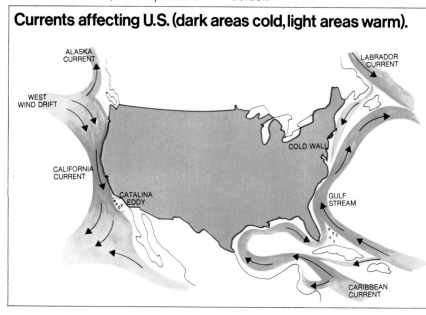

ALASKA CURRENT
WEST WIND DRIFT
CALIFORNIA CURRENT
CATALINA EDDY
LABRADOR CURRENT
COLD WALL
GULF STREAM
CARIBBEAN CURRENT

condenses and is deposited as ice crystals.

*Rain* is the most common form of precipitation. See: Weather forecast terminology—Showers.

*Snowfall* is not frozen rain, but ice crystals formed from water vapor. In order for it to form, the temperature in a cloud must be below freezing.

*Sleet* is frozen or partly frozen rain.

*Hail* is the result of the upward drift of air in thunderclouds. When the draft is strong enough, it either lifts freezing particles or delays their fall through successive layers of super-cooled clouds. This allows the particles to accumulate layers of ice and water. When the hailstones can no longer be kept aloft by updrafts, they fall to earth as lumps of ice.

*Graupel* is the same procedure as hail, but with snow formed into pellets.

**Radiation control.** Moisture in the air, as well as the time of the year, is an important control on the length and type of the growing period. Clouds and fog are widespread and effective insolation controls, and a determining factor of ground temperature and the total amount of light received during the season. Inland Spokane, for example, has greater measurements of both than overcast Seattle.

The differences can decide the types of commercial crops for a region, and whether its gardens are more suitable for foliage or flowering plants.

As clouds are not readily available radiation controls, a tree is a dependable substitute and is shade and can be put where you want it.

**Rain Gauge (Pluviometer or Udometer).** Vertical cylinder, open at top, located a safe distance from obstructions. U.S. Weather Service gauges normally use a funnel whose area at the top is exactly ten times the top of the tube beneath, providing greater accuracy in reading; in such gauges an inch of water in the tube. equals one tenth inch of rain. Automatic recording gauges operate by weight of the water. See page 85 for directions in making a home rain gauge.

**Seasons.** As it makes its annual trip around the sun, the earth also rotates on its axis to give us days and nights.

If this axis was perpendicular to the plane of the terrestial orbit, our weather patterns would be much less complex. We would have no seasons. Miami, New York, Fairbanks, Alaska, and Quito, Ecuador would all have

## Seasonal positions of Earth (note tilt of axis)

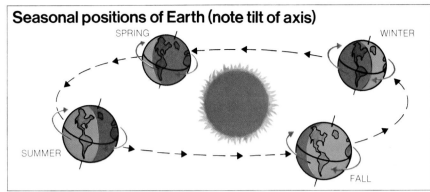

the same length days the year round. Daylight savings time could be abandoned.

As it is, the axis is tilted at 23½ degrees to its orbital plane and only the equatorial city experiences the same climate and day length through the year. In the other areas, only at the spring and fall equinoxes (about March 21 and September 23) bring days and nights of equal length.

The rest of the time, the axial slant results in unequal periods of daylight and darkness. The inequality is more pronounced with increasing distance north, culminating in 24 hours of total daylight at the pole during the summer solstice and 24 hours of relative darkness at the winter solstice. The same conditions, but reversed, occur in the southern hemisphere.

As the season progresses from winter toward summer, the sun appears higher in the sky as a given location moves to a more perpendicular angle of its radiation. The longer solar path at the loftier elevations also add to the daylight hours.

Summer is hotter than winter because the higher sun angle concentrates the solar energy, and longer days give the surface of a location more time to accumulate the radiation. Short nights lessen the the period of heat loss.

Away from marine temperature effects, cities in far northern locations record some high temperatures from the radiation gathered during the almost perpetual daylight. Fairbanks, at the edge of the arctic circle, can reach 100 degrees, and its average summer level is higher than that of fog-shrouded San Francisco.

**Smog.** A term coined in 1905 by a Dr. Des Voux to signify a mixture of smoke and fog; as yet neither technically defined nor adopted into a standard meteorological usage. The word is applied to the presence of chemical combinations that irritate the eyes and mucous membranes and cause plant damage. Although

fog is usually a forerunner during early morning hours its presence is not required. Sunshine brings about a chemical change that increases irritation when the fog evaporates, if any is present to begin with. The actual chemical make-up of smog is a problem that we are content to leave to the chemists.

**Solar energy (Insolation).** The all-important element controlling the winds, moisture distribution, atmospheric pressures, or any of the secondary factors contributing to our weather patterns.

Solar energy, the prime mover of all climatic behavior, is an awesome and impressive force. But it can be manipulated if we understand the principles of radiation—to increase it, decrease it, conserve it, or filter it to better meet our needs.

Most of our energy comes to earth in the form of short solar rays; a small fraction of it as long heat rays. When

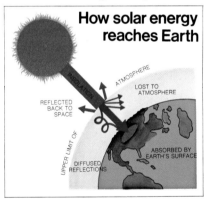

**How solar energy reaches Earth**

it reaches the upper limit of the atmosphere, about 1000 miles above us, about 25% of the insolation is reflected back into space.

Some more is lost on its passage through the atmosphere, but it picks up more power from the diffused reflections from dust particles and water vapor in the air. This action, of energy from other than direct sun rays, is an important source of heat. It explains why heat enters through glass walls on apparently sunless days, or why you can get such a sunburn at the beach in cloudy weather.

Insolation does not heat the air through which it travels, but the surface it strikes instead.

When they reach the earth, the rays are absorbed, or reflected back into the atmosphere, to a greater or lesser degree according to the composition of the surface receiving them.

After absorption, the energy is re-radiated as long rays. Short rays can penetrate the atmosphere, glass, or any transparent substance with ease. The long heat rays cannot.

Most are trapped by water vapor in the air, giving the earth tolerable days and nights compared to the temperature extremes of the relatively airless moon.

The height of this water vapor ceiling varies through the United States, because of temperature differences of the moisture sources.

The summer temperature of the Pacific Ocean is less than 60 degrees, that of the Gulf of Mexico, is around 80 degrees. Air takes up almost three times as much water over a warm ocean as a cold one, resulting in a vapor ceiling a half mile or more high in the far west. Influenced by the tropic airflows, the midwest, south, and east may have ceilings as low as 200 yards.

When the sun goes down, insolation stops and heat loss from the ground begins. Radiation is much faster to a cold high ceiling than a low warm one, and day-night temperatures under them can vary as much as 40 degrees.

Even though ground temperatures may be the same to begin with, guests at an outdoor Western barbecue usually have to don their sweaters early while those in other areas are comfortable in shirt-sleeves all evening.

Ceilings need not be water vapor, however. Foliage, canvas, plastic, or any other substance also serve the purpose and can be stationed at a low height to slow radiation and conserve heat.

During the day, some of the insolation is reflected back to the atmosphere, but a percentage is absorbed by the ground. In turn, this is re-radiated from the surface as long heat rays to warm the air. The net incoming radiation is greater than the outgoing, and ground becomes warmer.

At night the insolation is shut off, but the ground continues to radiate its heat. Net outgoing radiation is greater than incoming, and the ground cools.

**Terrain barriers (air mass diverters).** Standing like gigantic fences against the polar airflows, the massive mountain chains, the Cascades, the Sierra Nevada, and the Rockies tend to deflect much of the chilly air movement from the western areas, while the Appalachians afford pro-

## Terrain barriers

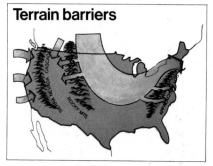

tection to parts of the eastern seaboard.

The irregular topography of the west is subject to a wider variety of climates than the flatter terrain of the east.

**Thunderheads.** Building of cumulus clouds, often resulting in precipitation;

## Breeze into thunderheads

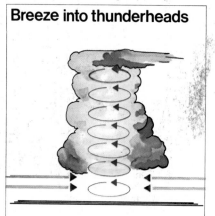

pressure areas below them pull adjacent air into their little whirling vortexes.

**Thunderstorms.** Result from violent vertical air movements, sometimes with a cloud-buildup exceeding 55,000 feet in elevation. The uplift may be caused by superheated ground surfaces, as in the midwest and east, or temperature differences between ocean and land, as in Florida and the southeast, or by frontal action.

In the west, they occur most frequently in the less stable air of higher mountain areas.

A thunderhead starts as a cumulus cloud (the billowy white favorites of photographers) but changes character as the air towers, expands and condenses to start precipitation.

Falling rain and ice cool the air, downdrafts shut off further ascending air to complete the storm's brief cycle. Steady winds in the upper atmosphere shape the cloud into the distinctive anvil top of the thunderhead.

Lightning, caused by the attraction of unlike electrical charges within the cloud, accompany thunderstorms. Similar attraction from the earth brings bolts to the surface, as charges from the ground respond to those from within the cloud. Thunder is the audible compression, or shock wave, caused by the collision of air replacing that consumed by lightning.

Lightning takes the path of least resistance, and tends to hit the highest places. Stay away from a lone tree in the open, from boats and the water. Ungrounded TV antennas are

## Typical air movement in thunderhead stages

40,000'

25,000'

BEGINNING          MATURE          DISSIPATING

dangerous, but if properly grounded act as lightning rods. Automobiles and steel-framed buildings are safe.

**Topography.** The surface features of a region—hills, valleys, rivers, lakes, canals, bridges, roads, cities. are important weather regulators. The western United States, including mountain ranges well over 10,000 feet high and valleys below sea level, experiences a far greater variety of climates than the relatively flat midwestern states. Some areas in the west are lushly forested, others are desert.

**Tornado.** A violent whirling wind. especially in the central United States, accompanied by a rapidly rotating, funnel-shaped cloud that usually destroys everything along its path.

**Tradewinds.** A wind that blows toward the equator from the northeast on the north side of the equator and from the southeast on the south side. See: Wind.

**Tropopause.** A transition zone between the troposphere and the stratosphere, at which the drop in temperature with increasing height ceases.

**Wind.** Any noticeable movement of air parallel to the earth's surface. Such a simple statement covers a tremendous range of climatic action and what it does to us.

It could be a pleasant breeze tempering a hot, midwestern afternoon, or a destructive hurricane battering a Florida coastline. In between, numberless variations affect us for better or worse.

Winds are of several different types. High above us flows a narrow, mysterious band of westerly wind, the jetstream. Discovered by American bomber pilots over the Pacific in World War II, it has since been a friend of aviators heading east and is avoided by those traveling in the opposite direction.

Jetstreams occur at overlaps in the tropopause, marking the upper limits of the atmospheric band closest to earth. Except that it speeds us faster to our destination on a stratospheric flight, however, we are without exact knowledge of its effect or non-effect upon us and our weather.

Sharing the higher atmosphere with the jet stream are the upper westerlies, circling the globe on undulating courses. They influence our climates from their lofty position by steering the high and low pressure areas, and the air masses, which bring our changing weather.

Surface winds, which impinge upon us most directly, might be grouped in three classes, for convenience rather than for meteorological terminology, to parallel our climatic nomenclature.

*I. Macrowinds* are established by the major climatic factors—solar radiation and the rotation of the earth. Their currents flow in fairly constant directions. They may change frequently and drastically from surface and seasonal effects, but always re-form, after disruption in their basic patterns, as the trade winds, the prevailing westerlies, or the polar easterlies.

Once set into motion by solar energy, the north-south circulation of the air is changed by the rotation of the earth.

This inexorable force is called by several names—the Coriolis Force, Ferrels' Law, or the Earth Deflective Force. By whichever term, it causes the flow to veer to its right in the northern hemisphere.

Not only air movement is affected. Major ocean currents swirl clockwise, rivers cut into their right banks, projectiles from cannons veer right-wise.

If so, why don't prevailing winds come from the same direction, rather than from both east and west?

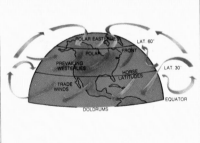

## Northern hemisphere prevailing wind patterns

The diagrams answer this question. Circulation begins at the equator, as heated air rises high above the earth and moves pole-ward. At about a third of the journey, it is deflecting slowly eastward. As more equatorial air arcs north and east, it piles up at this point to form a high pressure area at about latitude 30 degrees. Some air is forced back to the earth's surface again.

A portion flow south, drifting to its right as the "trade winds." Some flows north, veering right to form the "prevailing westerlies."

The remainder aloft continues north, cooling and contracting till it sinks to the surface near the pole. Pressure buildup in that region moves

it southward again, veering to its right to become the "polar easterlies."

At about 60 degrees latitude it collides with the westerlies along the "polar front", and resulting weather disturbances can reach as far south as Florida.

Regions of calm are established at the rising and subsiding zones of the circulation system. The equatorial "doldrums" and the "horse latitudes" were the dismay of skippers and crews in the days of sailing ships. The latter name apparently originated from the animals thrown overboard from becalmed vessels.

The captains also named the trade winds, as their steady courses marked a popular route to the west.

The prevailing westerlies blow on the latitudes which make them the dominant wind pattern of the United States.

*II. Mesowinds* blow from high and low pressure areas, veering according to the nature of the system. We can't do much about them, but we can take protective measures against the weather disturbances they cause or moderate them to some degree.

Highs develop wherever a large quantity of air accumulates and piles up, rather like an atmospheric mountain. They form usually over oceans, less frequently over colder land surfaces. All are huge, covering hundreds of thousands of square miles.

Lows are less dominant, smaller, and occur in the troughs between highs. They may be likened to moun-

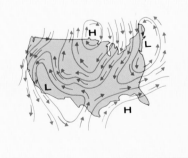

## Winds around high and low pressure areas

tain valleys. Air spirals from the high to the low, setting up the counter rotation.

Air is stable within the high, flows as water down its slope into the low, and sometimes breaks like a wave over the valley to create a full-fledged, whirling low-pressure cell.

Within the low the air is unstable, and under reduced pressure can rise rapidly to form clouds and precipitation.

**III. Microwinds** come from any direction, are caused by local ground heating and terrain, and are those most subject to our control. We can move in or out of them, lessen or increase them, or otherwise take advantage of or counteract them.

A diurnal event is a daily happening. While weather factors are too variable to make any of their manifestations absolutely certain, diurnal winds are regular enough to warrant the name.

Unequal heating of land and water surfaces are responsible for most of these local air movements. Transmission of heat by such methods is called convection (though the process is by no means limited to small diurnal winds).

At the seashore, the ocean temperature is constant, while that of adjacent land fluctuates during the day and night periods.

The land warms rapidly from solar radiation, the heated air rises. An onshore breeze begins when air from the cooler ocean flows inland to replace that ascending from the land.

At night the process is reversed, air from the cooling land moves toward the warmer ocean surface. The fresh breezes of the daytime action are usually more noticeable, however, than the offshore winds.

A large lake will set up the same type of circulation. On a minor scale, adjacent grassy fields and bare soil are subject to the same effects.

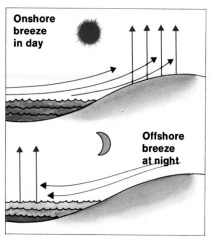

**Onshore breeze in day**

**Offshore breeze at night**

In rugged areas the upslope-downslope convectional winds can be even more pronounced. Mountains absorb heat more rapidly during daylight than nearby valleys, and lose it more rapidly at night.

The warm air rises swiftly, while that from below replaces it at increasing rate, its speed amplified by the confinement of canyon walls. At night it subsides even more rapidly, gathering power from the flow of tributary

canyons like a torrent of water, threatening the stability of campers' tents in Zion National Park and other recreational areas.

Local winds can blow wherever abnormal conditions create updrafts. The hotter city sucks in air from the cooler countryside. A forest fire creates even stronger air currents into it (the column of hot air can rise high enough into the upper atmosphere to start a firestorm, similar to thunderhead activity, but any precipitation caused is unlikely to reach the ground).

The most common visual evidences of the microwinds, though, are the tiny summer "dust devils," miniature tornados spun into motion by bubbles of hot air above them.

# Weather forecast terminology

The National Weather Service has made a careful study of terms used in forecasts, and the attempt is made to use terms having the same meaning as defined in a standard dictionary. Such terms as "unsettled," have in the past been little understood by the public, and their use is now discouraged. Brevity is essential because of widespread dissemination via telegraph and press wires, and because the important features may be overlooked in a more detailed forecast. There is a tendency among newscasters to edit the longer forecasts, which often changes their meaning. These definitions will help clarify the official forecasts:

**Broken clouds.** Aviation weather term for six to nine-tenths of sky covered with clouds, inclusive.

**Ceiling** (agricultural). Height of temperature inversion above ground. A term used in winter frost warnings to tell the citrus grower the depth of the cold air layer at the surface. Orchard heaters are most effective with a low ceiling, as the heat generated will not rise through the inversion into the layer of warmer air above it.

**Ceiling** (aviation). Height above ground of the lowest cloud layer covering more than half of the sky.

**Chance of.** Percentage of possibility not indicated. (Assumes less than a 50% chance of occurrence.)

**Clear.** Sky free or nearly free of clouds (less than one-tenth of sky covered). Does *not* refer to horizontal visibility, air pollution, haze, etc., although mariners often use the term

to denote "clear air," or good visibility.

**Clearing.** Cloudiness decreasing markedly (by at least 5/10) during forecast period.

**Degree day.** A departure of one degree per day in the mean daily temperature below an adopted standard reference temperature, usually 65°. (Used by heating engineers.)

**Drizzle.** Precipitation which consists of numerous tiny droplets which appear to float or fall slowly. Rarely associated with a real rain situation.

**Fair.** No precipitation, and sky covered by less than 4/10 low clouds.

**Fog.** A cloud formed at the surface of the earth and interfering with horizontal visibility at the surface. In Southern California coastal areas it is normally where the low cloud layer touches the ground. "Ground fog" may occur without the accompanying cloud layer, in which case the sky usually remains clear; this type is known technically as "radiation fog."

**Humidity.** State of the atmosphere with respect to water vapor content. It is measured in various ways, but the term in general use refers to *relative humidity*, which is the amount of actual moisture in the air compared to the amount required for saturation. It is computed in per cent of saturation; when the air is saturated the relative humidity is 100%, and fog or rain is most likely occurring. Less than 15% is considered very dry, and zero is never reached in the lower atmosphere. As warm air can hold more moisture than cool air, relative humidity varies inversely with changes in temperature; i.e., higher humidity occurs with lower temperature. A single figure for average relative humidity has little meaning unless it pertains to a specific time of day. Fog or dew on a cool morning will evaporate as the temperature rises and the humidity lowers.

**Intermittent.** Occurring at intervals; recurrent; periodic.

**Likely.** In all probability. Occurs in more than 50% of similar cases.

**Little temperature change.** Temperature change is not expected to be significant.

**Local.** Confined to a particular place or places; hence, not broad or general.

**Low clouds.** Term used to describe the cloud deck which occurs in the top of the moist layer of marine air when the clouds are *above* the ground level. Its technical name is Stratus Cloud, and is known in

Northern California as "high fog." It usually forms at night and dissipates during the forenoon over areas exposed to the sea air.

**Mostly sunny.** The prevailing condition will be sunny, but some clouds may be present, either over a portion of the area or for short periods of time.

**Occasional.** Occurring now and then; occurring at irregular intervals; the periods of precipitation are relatively short and occupy only a short part of the total time.

**Overcast.** More than nine-tenths of sky covered by clouds.

**Partial clearing.** A portion of the sky clearing.

**Partly cloudy.** Three-tenths to seven-tenths of sky covered by clouds.

**Perhaps.** More than 25% but less than 50% probability.

**Possibly.** Something may or may not occur. An event is neither probable nor impossible. Occurs in less than 25% of similar cases.

**Probably.** Reasonably but not certainly to be believed or expected; having more evidence for than against.

**Rain intensity.**

*Light rain:* Rate of fall less than .10 inch per hour or a 24-hour total of less than one inch.

*Moderate rain:* Rate of fall between .10 and .30 inch per hour or a 24-hour total from 1 to 2 inches.

*Heavy rain:* Rate of fall more than .30 inch per hour or a 24-hour total exceeding 2 inches.

**Scattered clouds.** In aviation weather, one to five-tenths of sky cover, inclusive.

**Showers.** Fall of rain of short duration and varying intensity, with periods of no rain (though not necessarily clearing) between showers.

**Sprinkles.** Occasional drops of rain; may be from a single cloud or from an overcast sky.

**Special shower terminology.**

| | Expected percent of area coverage |
|---|---|
| Risk of, chance of, few scattered showers | 0- 05 |
| Widely scattered showers | 15- 30 |
| Scattered showers | 30- 45 |
| Showers | 45- 75 |
| General showers (or rain) | 75-100 |

**Snow terminology and definitions.**

*Fluffy:* Large light feathery flakes.

*Powder:* Dry cold powdery snow; the perfect kind for all winter sports.

*Sticky:* Snow just beginning to melt; can be used by proper waxing of skis.

*Wet:* A soggy state between sticky and slush.

*Breakable:* A crust is "breakable" when it will not hold the full weight of a man on a single ski.

*Unbreakable icy:* A hard ice-like crust formed by freezing of a watery surface after a heavy thaw.

*Wind crust:* Formed by the action of wind on powder snow.

*Granular:* An old wet snow, in appearance and consistency much like the wet rock salt used to pack ice cream. Granular snow is usually found only in the spring and at high altitudes. Excellent for skiing.

*Corn:* Stage of snow between true granular and slush, existing only when air temperature is above freezing.

**Temperature.** Official temperatures are *shade* readings, taken in standard ventilated shelters in proper exposures—usually a few feet off the ground. Unofficial readings can vary widely, such as in direct sunlight or exposed to reflections of white buildings or concrete. Temperature *changes* in the forecast always refer to the same portion of the day, or to maximum or minimum temperatures; thus the term "warmer" or "cooler" does not refer to the normal change between day and night. The scale in common use is the *Fahrenheit,* in which freezing is 32 degrees and the boiling point is 212 degrees at sea level. For international and upper air use the *Celsius* or *Centigrade* scale is used, in each of which freezing is zero and the boiling point is 100 degrees at sea level. To convert from Centigrade to Fahrenheit, multiply by nine-fifths, or 1.8 and add 32; to change Fahrenheit to Centigrade (or Celsius), subtract 32 and multiply the result by five-ninths (5/9).

**Wind velocity.** Air movement measured in miles-per-hour or knots (nautical miles-per-hour). The approximate relation is 7 to 8 (seven knots equals eight miles-per-hour). To convert knots into m.p.h., add one-seventh; to change m.p.h. into knots, subtract one-eighth. Other scales are also used scientifically.

**Wind direction.** Direction *from which* the wind is blowing; i.e., a south wind is blowing from south to north. Directions relate to *True* north, or the geographic pole, except that aircraft and airport control towers use *Magnetic* directions relating to the magnetic pole, as do compasses.

# Reading the weather map

The National Weather Service maps compile and disseminate statistics gathered from stations and bureaus throughout the country. We usually see an adaptation of this information in the weather map of a newspaper, or on television broadcasts.

The most prominent features on such a map are whorling "isobars," lines connecting points of equal barometric pressure, and the frontal systems.

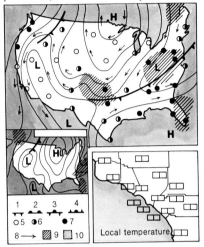

*1) cold front, 2) warm front, 3) stationary front, 4) occluded front, 5) clear, 6) partly cloudy, 7) cloudy, 8) wind direction, 9) rain, 10) snow.*

Isobars are labeled in inches of mercury (other maps might use millibars); initials 'L' and 'H' mark low and high pressure areas, arrows indicate wind directions around them. Winds are faster where isobars are closer together.

Its symbol shows a cold front advancing across the northwest, with cloudy skies at Seattle and Portland while Boise and Great Falls are partly cloudy. Another cold front is sweeping across the south, with rains in Texas. In the east, this has stalled against a warm front, becoming stationary and rainy.

The forecast for the following day shows the front now moving out to sea and leaving fair weather behind it.

Numbers adjacent to circles indicating cloud conditions are temperature readings of those locations. An additional map gives high and low temperatures of regional communities.

Other maps might report the conditions slightly differently, using specific symbols to describe precipitation, or Beaufort arrows for wind directions, but isobars and fronts are shown the same.

# Amateur weather watching

Without using instruments, any of us can become an amateur weather observer by cocking an eye to the sky and our surroundings. Look for signs familiar to sailors and farmers for an indication of what next to expect.

Of course, these signs are far from reliable unless you have observed them long enough to become familiar with their meanings and variations, but no beginning weatherman can expect too high a batting average. Even experts with professional equipment miss frequently.

On midwestern plains and flatter eastern terrain, the same general weather signs hold true over much of the region. Over the mountainous west they're subject to so many variations that accurate predictions are practically impossible from an overall standpoint.

To learn the conditions of any area, your best move is acquaintance with an old-timer who will pass his knowledge on to you. Or you can keep records over a period of time, noting what follows each weather change or precedes a storm.

By watching the skies and learning to read them, we can predict the weather by some of the methods of our forefathers.

"Evening red and morning gray,
Sets the traveler on his way;
Evening gray and morning red,
Brings rain down upon his head."

We've all heard this little jingle, or variations of it, but do you know its meaning?

The general circulation pattern moves the weather eastward. The red color is from the ball of the sun shining through dry atmosphere; gray means it's screened by moisture. A red sunset shows a storm has passed; a gray sunset that it's moving toward you.

Here are a few more indications of basic atmospheric conditions:

*Dew:* Heavy morning dew is a sign of a clear day. No dew may mean rain. (But this is subject to many variations from local conditions).

*Halo:* A halo around the sun or moon is formed by ice crystals in high cirrus clouds; indicates a warm front approach and possible rain. An old

saying advises counting the stars in a halo to predict the days before the storm's arrival.

One may mean the cloud layer is thick enough to hide others and rain is imminent. Many stars mean a thin layer with little moisture. A corona is caused by a middle altitude cloud layer of water particles.

*Moonlight:* In colder times of the year, this indicates a high sky ceiling and frosts are likely.

*Winds:* A veering wind, swinging clock-wise, is the sign of high pressure and fair weather. A counterclock-wise backing wind indicates low pressure and storm conditions.

*Rainbow:* A rainbow to the windward means rain is approaching; to the leeward rain is receding. Thus the proverb:

"Rainbow in morning,
Sailor take warning;
Rainbow at night,
Sailor's delight."

The band of the rainbow is formed by sunlight against the moisture of a storm, not through it.

*Lightning:* Flashes from the west or northwest mean the storm may reach you; lightning to the south or southeast will pass you.

Signs of a low pressure area (and possible storms) are birds roosting in flocks on fences, wires or beaches, smoke rising vertically, good visibility, when distant objects appear closer, and sticking doors and windows from the swelling of wood in greater humidity. (This is less noticeable with modern construction, but the pioneers could predict the weather by the creaking of their houses and furniture.)

## The meaning of cloud forms

The amateur weatherwatcher should learn the cloud forms and their meanings. These vary with locality. Many midwesterners, new to the Pacific coast, are fooled by the frequent layers of stratus clouds. Instead of the expected rain, they seldom progress beyond a high fog or slight drizzle.

Clouds are divided into groups. High clouds include the wispy cirrus, the milky sheet of cirro-stratus ("stratus" is a layer), and the rarer cirro-cumulus (mackerel sky); all form from ice crystals at 20,000-35,000 feet altitudes. Cirrus clouds don't precipitate, but may be a sign of an approaching warm front.

Middle clouds, 6500-20,000 feet high, are alto-cumulus, often separate little "woolpacks" at moderate alti-

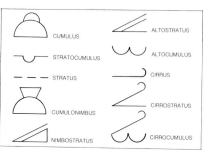

tudes, or alto-stratus, a fibrous gray sheet usually thick enough to cast a shadow. Water particles form these clouds.

Low clouds reach from 6500 feet to the ground. Strato-cumulus clouds resemble long parallel rolls pushed together, or are soft, gray, broken masses. Stratus is a low uniform layer, resembling fog but not resting on the ground, and may produce a drizzle. The nimbo-stratus is the low, dark, ragged cloud layer responsible for most of our precipitation.

(A nimbus, or rain-making cloud, is not classified by the single name any more but is combined with other forms.)

Clouds from vertical development are the billowy white cumulus of fair weather. These may, however, develop into the towering cumulo-nimbus, or thunderheads, the second greatest type of rainmakers.

Cumulus clouds are caused by local conditions, as rising warm air cools and condenses, and produce the short, hard, spotty summer showers. You can follow their buildup from their flat bases. The lower the base, and the earlier in the day it forms, the greater the chances of rain before evening. After the shower, the weather clears until the next buildup.

A well-marked alto-cumulus formation in the morning is a good sign of rain, but one in the late afternoon may dissipate before its precipitation point is reached.

Cumulus clouds may also indicate an approaching cold front, as the cold air pushes the warm air aloft like a snowplow, to cause a line of clouds accompanied by violent electrical effects. If you're in a small boat, head for shore to escape the violent winds of these line squalls.

The lingering storms of the warm fronts give ample notice before their arrival. Their first indication is a few cirrus, developing into cirro-stratus. By a second day, clouds may be alto-stratus with alto-cumulus edges. The next progression is low strato-cumulus to nimbo-cumulus and rain. Passing of a storm is marked by fleecy white cumulus against a clear sky, with fresh winds. Also see page 75.

# Home weather forecast station

From merely watching the weather, you may want to move to more accurate and scientific methods of measuring it. Important factors to check are wind direction and speed, temperature, humidity, air pressure, precipitation and cloud movement.

Instruments for measuring the various aspects of weather can be made from simple components outlined below. These are not as accurate as those marketed specifically for weather forecast and observation. Some gardening catalogues offer simple weather instruments.

Primitive Indian chieftains foretold coming rains by scalps hung in the wigwams, feeling the hair for its limpness or liveliness. A farmer hung a hemp cord in the barn, with a pointer to measure the humidity by the amount of the rope's contraction.

You may enjoy reading the magazine Weatherwise, published bimonthly by the Amateur Weathermen of America, Franklin Institute, Philadelphia 3, Pennsylvania. Membership in the organization, including a subscription to the magazine, costs $8.00 a year.

Records kept on a form sheet correlate your weather knowledge.

## Wind direction and speed

Scalps and barns are both less common today, but we can still use primitive methods of telling wind direction by the kicked-up dust, or noting the cold side of a wet finger held vertically (faster evaporation cools the windward side).

A windvane, however, is easily constructed from a few scrap materials. Locate it where wind is constant, avoid sites subject to eddies near buildings or trees. Mount it well above ground, as its friction slows wind velocity. Don't align the "north" indicator as shown by your compass, which points to magnetic rather than true north. Check the variation for your locality by a pilot's flight map or call the weather bureau, and adjust for the correction of degrees with a protractor.

An anemometer measures wind speed by revolutions of a wind-propelled assembly of rotating cups around a vertical axis. You can buy one, or make it and calibrate the speed by holding it outside a car window.

Count and record the revolutions at a given number of miles per hour for one minute against the wind, then with the wind. Average is half the total number. (Your anemometer, at 10 MPH, may turn 32 times against the wind and 18 with it, for a speed of 25 RPM in a simulated 10 MPH wind.)

By observation, you can estimate wind speed from the "Beaufort Scale of Wind Force," graduated by number

| BEAUFORT NUMBERS | M.P.H. | SYMBOL |
|---|---|---|
| 1 | 1-3 | ◎ |
| 2 | 4-7 | |
| 3 | 8-12 | |
| 4 | 13-18 | |
| 5 | 19-24 | |
| 6 | 25-31 | |
| 7 | 32-38 | |
| 8 | 39-46 | |
| 9 | 47-54 | |
| 10 | 55-63 | |
| 11 | 64-72 | |
| 12 | 73-82 | |

classifications according to wind action on ground objects. The weather service, mariners and aircraft most often use "knots," which are roughly 7/8 of the velocity in MPH. (Subtract an eighth for knots, add a seventh to convert to MPH.) (See page 86).

On a weather map, these forces are shown by "wind arrows" radiating from circles symbolizing cloud conditions. Winds approach from the directions toward which they radiate; their force is shown by the number of barbs on the tails of the arrows.

**How to estimate wind speeds.** Without an anemometer, you can determine the speed of the wind fairly accurately by using the Beaufort Scale of Wind Force with the U.S. Weather Bureau specifications for its use on land.

## Air temperature

Maximum and minimum recording thermometers provide high and low temperatures of a given period as well as the current readings. Mount them horizontally, in a shelter as protection from direct solar radiation, with good air circulation. Raise them at least five feet, away from radiating ground and wall surfaces.

A simple shelter is an apple box with one side knocked out, with the open side to the north. Mounting should hold the thermometer away from any radiation through the south side. Another shade layer a couple of inches above is additional radiation protection.

A more elaborate shelter is made with louvered sides and a lockable wire mesh door.

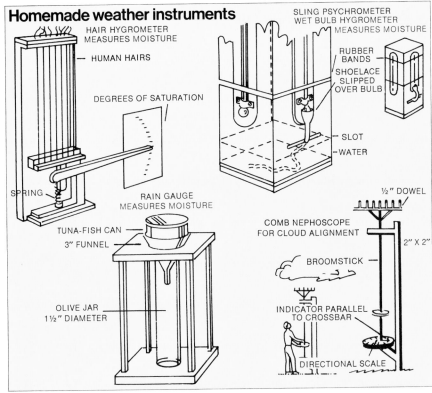

**Homemade weather instruments**

HAIR HYGROMETER MEASURES MOISTURE — HUMAN HAIRS — DEGREES OF SATURATION — SPRING

SLING PSYCHROMETER WET BULB HYGROMETER MEASURES MOISTURE — RUBBER BANDS — SHOELACE SLIPPED OVER BULB — SLOT — WATER

RAIN GAUGE MEASURES MOISTURE — TUNA-FISH CAN — 3" FUNNEL — OLIVE JAR 1½" DIAMETER

COMB NEPHOSCOPE FOR CLOUD ALIGNMENT — ½" DOWEL — 2" X 2" — BROOMSTICK — INDICATOR PARALLEL TO CROSSBAR — DIRECTIONAL SCALE

# Beaufort scale of wind force

| Beaufort Number | Miles per Hour | Knots | Terms Used in U.S.W.B. Forecasts | Wind Effects Observed on Land and at Sea |
|---|---|---|---|---|
| 0 . . . . | Less than 1 | Less than 1 | Light . . . . | Calm; smoke rises vertically; sea like mirror. |
| 1 . . . . | 1-3 | 1-3 | Light . . . . | Direction of wind shown by smoke drift but not by wind vanes; sea ripples with the appearance of scales formed, but without foam crests. |
| 2 . . . . | 4-7 | 4-6 | Light . . . . | Wind felt on face; leaves rustle; ordinary vane moved by wind. At sea, small wavelets, short but pronounced; crests appear glassy, do not break. |
| 3 . . . . | 8-12 | 7-10 | Gentle. . . . | Leaves and small twigs in constant motion; wind extends light flag. Large wavelets with crests beginning to break; foam appears glassy, perhaps scattered white horses (white foam crests). |
| 4 . . . . | 13-18 | 11-16 | Moderate . | Raises dust and loose paper; small branches are moved. Small waves, becoming longer; frequent white horses. |
| 5 . . . . | 19-24 | 17-21 | Fresh . . . . | Small trees in leaf begin to sway; crested wavelets form on inland waters. Moderate waves of a pronounced long form at sea; many white horses, possibly some spray. |
| 6 . . . . | 25-31 | 22-27 | Strong . . . | Large branches in motion; whistling heard in telegraph wires; umbrellas used with difficulty. Large waves begin to form; white foam crests more extensive everywhere; probably some spray. |
| 7 . . . . | 32-38 | 28-33 | Strong . . . | Whole trees in motion; inconvenience felt walking against wind. Sea heaps up; some white foam from breaking waves blows in streaks with the wind. |
| 8 . . . . | 39-46 | 34-40 | Gale . . . . | Breaks twigs off trees; generally impedes progress. Moderately high waves. Edges of crests beginning to break into spindrift; well-marked streaks of foam blow along direction of wind. |
| 9 . . . . | 47-54 | 41-47 | Gale . . . . | Slight structural damage occurs (chimney pots, slates removed). High waves, dense streaks of foam along direction of wind; spray may affect visibility. |
| 10 . . . | 55-63 | 48-55 | Whole gale . | Seldom experienced inland; trees uprooted; considerable structural damage occurs. Very high waves with long overhanging crests; great patches of foam blow in dense white streaks along direction of wind. Sea surface takes on a white appearance; visibility affected. |
| 11 . . . . | 64-72 | 58-63 | Whole gale . | Very rarely experienced; accompanied by widespread damage. Exceptionally high waves; sea completely covered with long white patches of foam lying along direction of wind; edges of wave crests everywhere blown into froth. Visibility affected. |
| 12 . . . . | 73 or more | 64 or more | Hurricane . | Very rarely experienced; accompanied by widespread damage. Air filled with foam and spray; sea completely white with driving spray. Visibility very seriously affected. |

## Measuring moisture in the air

A hygrometer measures the humidity of the air (an updated version of the chieftain's weather-scalp). You can make your own from human hair (blond is best) but commercial types are inexpensive and record the percent of humidity on a dial.

The sling psychrometer is an alternate instrument to the hygrometer. You can make your own with two thermometers. Encase the lower end of one in a bootlace, dip it in water, and whirl the instrument a few times to stimulate evaporation before a comparative reading. The wet bulb temperature is lower than the dry, varying with the humidity of the air. You'll need a psychrometer table to convert the readings to the relative humidity.

The dewpoint, where saturation (dew, fog or rain) occurs, is approached as the two readings draw closer together.

Humidity instruments may be mounted in the shelter with the thermometer.

## Air pressure

Meteorologists use mercurial barometers to measure air pressure, which record its weight against a tube of mercury. Their readings are converted to millibars by multiplying by 33.864.

Most home models are the less accurate but more convenient aneroid types, which indicate air pressure against an airless container on a dial. It may read as inches of mercury, millibars or both. (Average sea level pressure, 29.92 inches, is equivalent to 1013.2 millibars).

As air pressure is the same indoors or out, unless you're suddenly caught in a tornado, the barometer may be stationed in the house. An airplane altimeter is a type of barometer whose readings change with altitude and lessening air pressure. Your home readings will also be lower as your altitude above sea level increases.

You can make your own simple barometer with a pointer glued to the top of an air-tight, rubber-capped glass container. Changing air pressures expand or contract the rubber, moving the pointer across a dial.

The early Cape Cod weather glass operated on the same principle. Air trapped inside the container pushed liquid through the spout as outside pressure lessened.

A falling barometer indicates an approaching low pressure area and possible storms; a rising one means high pressure and fair weather is on the way.

## Recording rainfall

A rain gauge shows the amount of precipitation. Locate it high enough to avoid ground splashes, away from dripping plants, eaves or obstacles which cause wind eddies.

Gauges given away as advertising promotion by commercial firms will usually serve the purpose, or you can buy a more professional model.

You can make one of a funnel set in the mouth of a large can, to channel water into a tall, narrow glass container below. Calibrate its measurement by water levels indicated when measured and poured by a commercial gauge. Correct amount will be area across container over area at top of funnel times measured depth in container.

### Direction of cloud movement

Winds aloft do not always correspond to those at the surface, but a nephoscope will indicate their direction by movements clouds aligned along its longitudinal axis. An easily made instrument is suitable for very rough comparative calculations. Knowing approximate heights of cloud formations, their passage over the cross-bars estimates wind speed.

## Homemade weather instruments

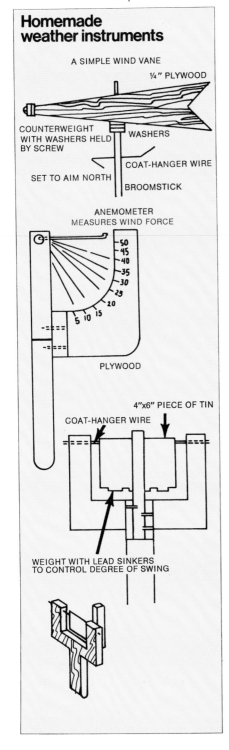

A SIMPLE WIND VANE

¼" PLYWOOD

COUNTERWEIGHT WITH WASHERS HELD BY SCREW

WASHERS

SET TO AIM NORTH

COAT-HANGER WIRE

BROOMSTICK

ANEMOMETER
MEASURES WIND FORCE

PLYWOOD

4"x6" PIECE OF TIN

COAT-HANGER WIRE

WEIGHT WITH LEAD SINKERS TO CONTROL DEGREE OF SWING

# Learning metric measures

Soon the weather man will report wind velocity in kilometers and rainfall in centimeters. The United States Senate has unanimously voted to adopt the Metric System as used by the rest of the world. Conversion will take place gradually over the next 10 years.

It is a good idea to begin to acquaint yourself with some of the more familiar terms that will be useful for gardeners. Prepare to measure garden rows in meters, mix spray solutions based on milliters per liter, buy seed in grams and record temperature in Celsius degrees.

Metric is based on the decimal system. It is easy to learn and will eventually save time and confusion. It is simply a 10-unit progression system and contains only six basic units: meter (length); kilogram (weight); degree (Celsius temperature); second (time); ampere (electrical current); and candela (light intensity).

Prefixes in the metric system have the same meaning whether measuring length, volume or mass.

### Common prefixes
(to be used with basic units)

| | |
|---|---|
| **Milli:** | one-thousandth (0.001) |
| **Centi:** | one-hundredth (0.01) |
| **Deci:** | one-tenth (0.1) |
| **Kilo:** | one-thousand times (1000) |
| **Hecto:** | one-hundred times (100) |
| **Decka:** | ten times (10) |

Conversion between metric units is accomplished by simply moving the decimal point to the right or left.

### Other commonly used units

| | |
|---|---|
| **Millimeter:** | 0.0001 meter; diameter of paper clip wire |
| **Centimeter:** | 0.01 meter; width of a paper clip (about 0.4 inch) |
| **Kilometer:** | 1000 meters; somewhat further than ½ mile (about 0.6 mile) |
| **Kilogram:** | 1000 grams; a little more than 2 pounds (about 2.2 pounds) |
| **Milliliter:** | 0.001 liter; five of them make a teaspoon |

### Other useful units

| | |
|---|---|
| **Hectare:** | about 2½ acres |
| **Tonne:** | about one ton |

### Approximate common equivalents
(U.S. to Metric)

| | |
|---|---|
| **1 cubic inch** | = 16.0 cubic centimeters |
| **1 cubic foot** | = 0.03 cubic meter |
| **1 cubic yard** | = 0.76 cubic meter |
| **1 teaspoon** | = 5.0 milliliters |
| **1 tablespoon** | = 15.0 milliliters |
| **1 fluid ounce** | = 30.0 milliliters |
| **1 cup** | = 0.24 liter |
| **1 pint** | = 0.47 liter |
| **1 quart (liquid)** | = 0.95 liter |
| **1 gallon (liquid)** | = 0.004 cubic meter |
| **1 peck** | = 0.009 cubic meter |
| **1 bushel** | = 0.04 cubic meter |

For more information, write to:
Metric Information Office
National Bureau of Standards
Washington, DC 20234
or secure list of publications on the subject from:
Superintendent of Documents
US Government Printing Office
Washington, DC 20402

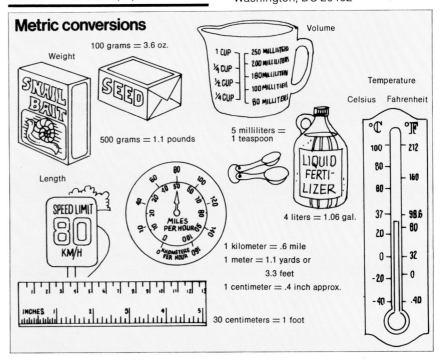

## Metric conversions

Weight

100 grams = 3.6 oz.

500 grams = 1.1 pounds

Length

SPEED LIMIT 80 KM/H

MILES PER HOUR

KILOMETERS PER HOUR

INCHES 1 2 3 4 5

Volume

1 CUP — 250 MILLILITERS
¾ CUP — 200 MILLILITERS
½ CUP — 180 MILLILITERS
½ CUP — 100 MILLILITERS
¼ CUP — 80 MILLILITERS

5 milliliters = 1 teaspoon

LIQUID FERTILIZER

4 liters = 1.06 gal.

1 kilometer = .6 mile
1 meter = 1.1 yards or 3.3 feet
1 centimeter = .4 inch approx.

30 centimeters = 1 foot

Temperature

Celsius    Fahrenheit

°C        °F
100 — 212
80 — 160
80
37 — 98.6
      80
20
0 — 32
-20 — 0
-40 — -40

# Planting dates are made of rubber

It's been our experience that the vegetable gardener begins to know how to make the most of the climate of his garden after a year or two of trial and error plantings and faithful record keeping. Here we give you a starting point.

You can get a general fix on your climate and establish a pattern for your planting this way: take a look at the chart opposite showing the normal time to plant in the April to October growing season in relation to last and first frost dates. The sequence is based on the premise that cool weather crops need cool weather to mature in and warm weather crops need warm weather; that it is sometimes easier to find a cool ripening period in the fall than in the spring; that in some climates the cool period is in the winter months.

The basic plan is to start the hardy cool weather crops so they will mature *before* hot weather; to plant the warm weather crops when the weather warms and take advantage of the cool days of fall by planting in late summer or early fall depending on the length of growing season. If cool and warm weather designation is new to you, see the vegetable chart on pages 90, 91.

Knowing the weather preference of each vegetable it should be easy to fit it into the growing season of your garden—those days between the last frost of spring and the first frost of fall. In the bar chart on the following page we show the length of the growing season for representative cities of the North, (your climate will be similar to one of them). When you analyze the bar chart you realize that the length-of-growing season is sometimes a poor clue to your climate in terms of vegetable production.

Beating the averages, planting earlier or later than a sensible person should, has its rewards. One freak early freeze may cut short the late planted beans and corn one year out of three, but out-of-season vegetables in the other years make up for the one failure.

You can't do much about the big overall climate but you can do a lot with the microclimates in your garden. You can make a warm area warmer by a wind-break, or bring in more sunlight by thinning out overgrown trees. You can lengthen the growing season by planting in raised beds with a soil that drains quickly and warms up early in the spring.

The container gardener can enjoy a much longer growing season than the dirt gardener. There's no waiting period for the soil to dry. Pots and boxes can be moved to give protection from frost at night and into a warm spot during the day.

For many a home gardener in areas where the last and first frost dates measure the growing season these dates seem to be made of rubber. A 200 day growing season may be 220 one year and 160 the next. "Last frost dates" published by the weather bureau are "normal" or "mean" dates. It's a date half way between the earliest and latest frost date of the spring season. There's a 50% chance that it will come earlier or later.

## Make the most of the swing of the seasons

This chart of seasonal planting dates was prepared for the growing seasons of Long Island, New York. In principle it applies to all areas where the last frost date in spring is in April and the first frost date of autumn in October. Planting for fall and winter crops extends the harvest.

### Early Spring
**Plant as soon as ground can be worked in spring**
Broccoli plants • Cabbage plants • Endive
Kohlrabi • Lettuce • Onion sets • Parsley
Peas • Radishes • Spinach • Turnips

### Mid-Spring
**Plant these at time of the average last killing frost**
Carrots • Cauliflower plants • Beets
Onion seeds • Parsnips • Swiss Chard
**Plant two weeks later:**
Beans • Corn • Potatoes, early
Tomato seeds

### Early Summer
**Plant when soil and weather are warm**
Beans, Lima • Cantaloupe • Celery plants
Crenshaw melons • Cucumbers
Eggplant plants • Pumpkins • Pepper plants
Potatoes for winter • Squash • Tomato plants
Watermelons

### Mid-Summer-Fall
**Plant in late June or early July**
Beets • Broccoli • Cabbage • Cauliflower
Kohlrabi • Lettuce • Radishes
Spinach • Turnips

# Growing Season Climate

| Station | Growing Season Days | July Max./Min. Temp. | % of Sunshine | Inches of Rain | Days of Rain | Comments | Max./Min. Temp. (Dec.) |
|---|---|---|---|---|---|---|---|
| Duluth, Minn. | 125 | 79/53 | 68 | 14" | 42 | Short Cool | 24/5 |
| Bismarck, N. Dak. | 136 | 86/58 | 73 | 10" | 43 | Short Mild | 27/9 |
| Sault Ste. Marie | 138 | 76/54 | 63 | 14" | 50 | Short Cool | 27/14 |
| Concord, N.H. | 142 | 83/56 | 57 | 15" | 47 | Short Mild | 35/15 |
| Burlington, Vt. | 148 | 82/56 | 62 | 19" | 57 | Short Mild | 30/13 |
| Rapid City, S. Dak. | 150 | 88/60 | 73 | 9" | 45 | Mild Dry | 39/16 |
| Montreal, Que. | 155 | 78/61 | 60 | 13" | 44 | Short Cool | 26/13 |
| Quebec, Que. | 156 | 76/57 | 56 | 12" | 42 | Short Cool | 22/9 |
| N. Platte, Neb. | 160 | 90/62 | 78 | 10" | 44 | Mild Dry | 40/14 |
| Green Bay, Wis. | 161 | 82/59 | 70 | 15" | 44 | Mild Short | 29/15 |
| Minneapolis, Minn | 166 | 84/61 | 72 | 17" | 55 | Mild Short | 27/9 |
| Sioux City, Iowa | 167 | 90/65 | 75 | 17" | 52 | Mild Short | 34/15 |
| Albany, N.Y. | 169 | 84/60 | 63 | 15" | 59 | Mild Humid | 34/18 |
| Portland, Me. | 169 | 80/57 | 62 | 17" | 56 | Cool Damp | 35/16 |
| Springfield, Mass. | 171 | 84/60 | 63 | 17" | 60 | Mild Humid | 36/19 |
| Madison, Wis. | 177 | 82/60 | 70 | 19" | 56 | Mild Humid | 30/14 |
| Buffalo, N.Y. | 179 | 80/59 | 70 | 17" | 61 | Cool Damp | 34/21 |
| Hartford, Conn. | 180 | 85/62 | 62 | 21" | 60 | Mild Humid | 38/20 |
| Detroit, Mich. | 181 | 84/65 | 69 | 17" | 59 | Mild Humid | 32/24 |
| Des Moines, Ia. | 183 | 87/65 | 75 | 21" | 56 | Mild Humid | 34/17 |
| Dodge City, Kans. | 184 | 93/68 | 78 | 14" | 49 | Warm Dry | 46/24 |
| Toronto, Ont. | 186 | 79/59 | 70 | 12" | 47 | Cool Damp | 33/21 |
| Pittsburgh, Pa. | 186 | 85/65 | 64 | 20" | 64 | Mild Humid | 40/26 |
| Dover, Dela. | 188 | 85/68 | 64 | 25" | 57 | Mild Humid | 44/28 |
| Boston, Mass. | 192 | 82/65 | 64 | 21" | 62 | Mild Humid | 40/26 |
| Chicago, Ill. | 192 | 84/67 | 73 | 21" | 60 | Mild Humid | 36/22 |
| Indianapolis, Ind. | 193 | 86/64 | 74 | 23" | 59 | Mild Humid | 37/23 |
| Charleston, W.V. | 193 | 86/64 | 60 | 24" | 70 | Mild Humid | 46/29 |
| Cleveland, Ohio | 195 | 82/61 | 72 | 20" | 67 | Mild Humid | 37/24 |
| Columbus, Ohio | 196 | 87/63 | 71 | 21" | 57 | Mild Humid | 40/23 |
| Topeka, Kans. | 200 | 92/68 | 78 | 24" | 59 | Warm Humid | 43/24 |
| Washington, D.C. | 201 | 87/69 | 64 | 25" | 60 | Mild Humid | 46/30 |
| Springfield, Ill. | 205 | 90/66 | 76 | 24" | 64 | Warm Humid | 40/24 |
| Kansas City, Mo. | 209 | 92/71 | 76 | 25" | 61 | Warm Humid | 44/28 |
| Evansville, Ind. | 211 | 90/67 | 78 | 24" | 63 | Warm Humid | 45/28 |
| New Brnswck, N.J. | 211 | 85/67 | 65 | 26" | 67 | Mild Humid | 42/28 |
| N.Y.C., N.Y. | 219 | 85/68 | 66 | 26" | 69 | Mild Humid | 42/30 |
| St. Louis, Mo. | 220 | 89/67 | 72 | 24" | 64 | Warm Humid | 43/26 |
| Phila. Pa. | 232 | 86/65 | 64 | 28" | 71 | Mild Humid | 42/26 |
| Cairo, Ill. | 233 | 90/72 | 82 | 26" | 70 | Warm Humid | 46/33 |

Month column headers across the table: JAN. | FEB. | MAR. | APR. | MAY | JUNE | JULY | AUG. | SEPT. | OCT. | NOV. | DEC.

# Use of planting chart

"Depth to plant seed." A quick look at the fractions and you know that many gardeners plant too deep.

"Number of seed to sow per foot." It's one answer to the question "How thick or thin should I sow seeds?" Our figures give the average of 6 expert seed-sowers—3 pessimists and 3 optimists.

"Distance between plants." First figure is minimum. You get better growth at wider spacing. You cut down on the competition.

"Distance between rows." The minimum distance assumes that space is limited and weeding will be done by hand tools. Wider distance between rows is preferable and if power equipment is used, necessary.

"Number of days to germination." Number of days varies by soil temperature. Early spring sowings will take longer than later plantings. We give the range to answer questions like this one: "How long do I wait before I know I have to reseed?"

"Soil temperatures for seed." Seeds that "require cool soil" do best in a temperature range of 50°-65°; that "tolerate cool soil" in a 50°-85° range; those that "require warm soil in a 65°-85° range.

"Weeks needed to grow to transplant size." The variation of 4-6, 5-7, 10-12 weeks allows for hot-bed, greenhouse, and window sill, and under grow-lamp conditions. Generally the warmer the growing conditions the shorter the time to grow transplants.

"Days to maturity." Figures in this column show the *relative* length of time needed to grow a crop from seed or transplant to table use. The time will vary by variety and season.

| Vegetable | Depth to plant seed (inches) | Number of seed to sow per foot | Distance between plants (inches) | Distance between rows (inches) | Number of days to germination | Needs cool soil | Tolerates cool soil | Needs warm soil | Weeks needed to grow to transplant size | Days to maturity | Remarks |
|---|---|---|---|---|---|---|---|---|---|---|---|
| Artichoke | ½ | | 60 | 72 | 7-14 | | • | | 4-6 | 1 year | Start with divisions preferred. |
| Asparagus | 1½ | | 18 | 36 | 7-21 | | • | | 1 year | 3 years | Sow in spring and transplant the following spring. |
| Beans: Snap Bush | 1½-2 | 6-8 | 2-3 | 18-30 | 6-14 | | | • | | 45-65 | Make sequence plantings. |
| Snap Pole | 1½-2 | 4-6 | 4-6 | 36-48 | 6-14 | | | • | | 60-70 | Long bearing season if kept picked. |
| Lima Bush | 1½-2 | 5-8 | 3-6 | 24-30 | 7-12 | | | • | | 60-80 | Needs warmer soil than snap beans. |
| Lima Pole | 1½-2 | 4-5 | 6-10 | 30-36 | 7-12 | | | • | | 85-90 | |
| Fava—Broadbean Winsor Bean | 2½ | 5-8 | 3-4 | 18-24 | 7-14 | | • | | | 80-90 | Hardier than the common bean. |
| Garbanzo—Chick Pea | 1½-2 | 5-8 | 3-4 | 24-30 | 6-12 | | | • | | 105 | |
| Scarlet Runner | 1½-2 | 4-6 | 4-6 | 36-48 | 6-14 | | | • | | 60-70 | Will grow in cooler summers than common beans. |
| Soybean | 1½-2 | 6-8 | 2-3 | 24-30 | 6-14 | | | • | | 55-85 95-100 | Choose varieties to fit your climate. See text. |
| Beets | ½-1 | 10-15 | 2 | 12-18 | 7-10 | | • | | | 55-65 | Thin out extra plants and use for greens. |
| Black-eye Cowpea Southern Peas | ½-1 | 5-8 | 3-4 | 24-30 | 7-10 | | | • | | 65-80 | |
| Yardlong Bean Asparagus Bean | ½-1 | 2-4 | 12-24 | 24-36 | 6-13 | | | • | | 65-80 | Variety of Black eye peas. Grow as pole bean. |
| Broccoli, sprouting | ½ | 10-15 | 14-18 | 24-30 | 3-10 | | • | | 5-7* | 60-80T | 80-100 days from seed. |
| Brussels Sprouts | ½ | 10-15 | 12-18 | 24-30 | 3-10 | | • | | 4-6* | 80-90T | 100-110 days from seed. |
| Cabbage | ½ | 8-10 | 12-20 | 24-30 | 4-10 | | • | | 5-7* | 65-95T | Use thinnings for transplants. 90-150 days from seed. |
| Cabbage, Chinese | ½ | 8-16 | 10-12 | 18-24 | 4-10 | | • | | 4-6 | 80-90 | Best as seeded fall crop. |
| Cardoon | ½ | 4-6 | 18 | 36 | 8-14 | | • | | 8 | 120-150 | Transplanting to harvest about 90 days. |
| Carrot | ¼ | 15-20 | 1-2 | 14-24 | 10-17 | | • | | | 60-80 | Start using when ½" in diameter to thin stand. |
| Cauliflower | ½ | 8-10 | 18 | 30-36 | 4-10 | | • | | 5-7* | 55-65T | 70-120 days from seed. |
| Celeriac | ⅛ | 8-12 | 8 | 24-30 | 9-21 | • | | | 10-12* | 90-120T | Keep seeds moist. |
| Celery | ⅛ | 8-12 | 8 | 24-30 | 9-21 | • | | | 10-12* | 90-120T | Keep seeds moist. |
| Celtuce—Asparagus Lettuce | ½ | 8-10 | 12 | 18 | 4-10 | | • | | 4-6 | 80 | Same culture as lettuce. |
| Chard, Swiss | 1 | 6-10 | 4-8 | 18-24 | 7-10 | | • | | | 55-65 | Use thinnings for early greens. |
| Chicory—Witloof (Belgian Endive) | ¼ | 8-10 | 4-8 | 18-24 | 5-12 | | • | | | 90-120 | Force mature root for Belgian Endive. |
| Chives | ½ | 8-10 | 8 | 10-16 | 8-12 | | • | | | 80-90 | Also propagate by division of clumps. |
| Collards | ¼ | 10-12 | 10-15 | 24-30 | 4-10 | | • | | 4-6* | 65-85T | Direct seed for a fall crop. |
| Corn, Sweet | 2 | 4-6 | 10-14 | 30-36 | 6-10 | | | • | | 60-90 | Make successive plantings. |
| Corn Salad | ½ | 8-10 | 4-6 | 12-16 | 7-10 | | • | | | 45-55 | Tolerant of cold weather. |
| Cress, Garden | ¼ | 10-12 | 2-3 | 12-16 | 4-10 | | • | | | 25-45 | Seeds sensitive to light. |
| Cucumber | 1 | 3-5 | 12 | 48-72 | 6-10 | | | • | 4 | 55-65 | See text about training. |
| Dandelion | ½ | 6-10 | 8-10 | 12-16 | 7-14 | | • | | | 70-90 | |
| Eggplant | ¼-½ | 8-12 | 18 | 36 | 7-14 | | | • | 6-9* | 75-95T | |

*Transplants preferred over seed.

T Number of days from setting out transplants; all others are from seeding.

| Vegetable | Depth to plant seed (inches) | Number of seed to sow per foot | Distance between plants (inches) | Distance between rows (inches) | Number of days to germination | Soil temperature for seed | | | Weeks needed to grow to transplant size | Days to maturity | Remarks |
|---|---|---|---|---|---|---|---|---|---|---|---|
| | | | | | | Needs cool soil | Tolerates cool soil | Needs warm soil | | | |
| Endive | ½ | 4-6 | 9-12 | 12-24 | 5-9 | | • | | 4-6 | 60-90 | Same culture as lettuce. |
| Wonder Berry Garden Huckleberry | ½ | 8-12 | 24-36 | 24-36 | 5-15 | | | • | 5-10 | 60-80 | |
| Fennel, Florence | ½ | 8-12 | 6 | 18-24 | 6-17 | | • | | | 120 | Plant in fall in mild winter areas. |
| Garlic | 1 | | 2-4 | 12-18 | 6-10 | | • | | | 90-sets | |
| Ground Cherry Husk Tomato | ½ | 6 | 24 | 36 | 6-13 | | | • | 6* | 90-100T | Treat same as tomatoes. |
| Horseradish | Div. | | 10-18 | 24 | | | • | | | 6-8 mth. | Use root division 2-8" long. |
| Jerusalem Artichoke | Tubers 4 | | 15-24 | 30-60 | | | • | | | 100-105 | |
| Kale | ½ | 8-12 | 8-12 | 18-24 | 3-10 | | • | | 4-6 | 55-80 | Direct seed for fall crop. |
| Kohlrabi | ½ | 8-12 | 3-4 | 18-24 | 3-10 | | • | | 4-6 | 60-70 | |
| Leeks | ½-1 | 8-12 | 2-4 | 12-18 | 7-12 | | • | | 10-12 | 80-90T | 130-150 days from seed. |
| Lettuce: Head | ¼-½ | 4-8 | 12-14 | 18-24 | 4-10 | • | | | 3-5 | 55-80 | Keep seed moist. |
| Leaf | ¼-½ | 8-12 | 4-6 | 12-18 | 4-10 | • | | | 3-5 | 45-60 | Keep seed moist. |
| Muskmelon | 1 | 3-6 | 12 | 48-72 | 4-8 | | | • | 3-4 | 75-100 | |
| Mustard | ½ | 8-10 | 2-6 | 12-18 | 3-10 | | • | | | 40-60 | Use early to thin. |
| Nasturtium | ½-1 | 4-8 | 4-10 | 18-36 | | | • | | | 50-60 | |
| Okra | 1 | 6-8 | 15-18 | 28-36 | 7-14 | | | • | | 50-60 | |
| Onion: sets | 1-2 | | 2-3 | 12-24 | | | • | | | 95-120 | Green onions 50-60 days. |
| plants | 2-3 | | 2-3 | 12-24 | | | • | | 8 | 95-120T | |
| seed | ½ | 10-15 | 2-3 | 12-24 | 7-12 | | • | | | 100-165 | |
| Parsley | ¼-½ | 10-15 | 3-6 | 12-20 | 14-28 | | • | | 8 | 85-90 | |
| Parsnips | ½ | 8-12 | 3-4 | 16-24 | 15-25 | | • | | | 100-120 | |
| Peas | 2 | 6-7 | 2-3 | 18-30 | 6-15 | • | | | | 65-85 | |
| Peanut | 1½ | 2-3 | 6-10 | 30 | | | | • | | 110-120 | Requires warm growing season. |
| Peppers | ¼ | 6-8 | 18-24 | 24-36 | 10-20 | | | • | 6-8 | 60-80T | |
| Potato | 4 | 1 | 12 | 24-36 | 8-16 | | • | | | 90-105 | |
| Pumpkin | 1-1½ | 2 | 30 | 72-120 | 6-10 | | | • | | 70-110 | Give them room. |
| Purslane | ½ | 6-8 | 6 | 12 | 7-14 | | • | | | | |
| Radish | ½ | 14-16 | 1-2 | 6-12 | 3-10 | • | | | | 20-50 | Early spring or late fall weather. |
| Rhubarb | Crown | | 36 | 60 | | | • | | | | Matures 2nd season. |
| Rocket | ¼ | 8-10 | 8-12 | 18-24 | 7-14 | | • | | | 80-90 | |
| Rutabaga | ½ | 4-6 | 8-12 | 18-24 | 3-10 | | • | | | 80-90 | |
| Salsify | ½ | 8-12 | 2-3 | 16-18 | | | • | | | 110-150 | |
| Salsify, Black | ½ | 8-12 | 2-3 | 16-18 | | | • | | | 110-150 | |
| Shallot | Bulb—1 | | 2-4 | 12-18 | | | • | | | 60-75 | |
| Spinach | ½ | 10-12 | 2-4 | 12-14 | 6-14 | • | | | | 40-65 | |
| Malabar | ½ | 4-6 | 12 | 12 | 10 | | • | | | 70 | |
| New Zealand | 1½ | 4-6 | 18 | 24 | 5-10 | | • | | | 70-80 | |
| Tampala | ¼-½ | 6-10 | 4-6 | 24-30 | | | | • | | 21-42 | Thin and use early while tender. |
| Squash (summer) | 1 | 4-6 | 16-24 | 36-60 | 3-12 | | | • | | 50-60 | |
| Squash (winter) | 1 | 1-2 | 24-48 | 72-120 | 6-10 | | | • | | 85-120 | |
| Sunflower | 1 | 2-3 | 16-24 | 36-48 | 7-12 | | | • | | 80-90 | Space wide for large heads. |
| Sweet Potato | Plants | | 12-18 | 36-48 | | | | • | | 120 | Propagate from cuttings. |
| Tomato | ½ | | 18-36 | 36-60 | 6-14 | | | • | 5-7 | 55-90T | Early var. 55-60. Mid 65-75, Late 80-100. |
| Turnip | ½ | 14-16 | 1-3 | 15-18 | 3-10 | • | | | | 45-60 | Thin early for greens. |
| Watermelon | 1 | | 12-16 | 60 | 3-12 | | | • | | 80-100 | Ice-box size mature earlier. |

*Transcription preferred over seed.

T Number of days from setting out transplants; all others are from seeding.

# People, climate and plants

When you map the home towns of the members of some plant societies you get a rough picture of the adaptability of the plant and the gardeners' reaction to it.

A plant that gets its own "society" must have a special relationship to people. This relationship is generally due to the multiplicity of species and varieties to be found under such names as Primrose, Camellia, Rhododendron, Iris, Hosta and others.

There's a mystery about these plants that is never completely solved. There seems always to be a new discovery in the plant's infinite variations. They challenge the inquisitive and call for the pooling of experiences through a society.

Climate is, of course, the major factor in the distribution of plants but there are other factors. The interest that people have in a plant has much to do with its distribution. One enthusiastic hobbyist may influence dozens of gardeners to see the plants as he sees them.

When you consider the primrose in all of its sections, species and varieties the ideal climate is in the cool, moist section of western Washington, Oregon and northern California. As other areas approach these soil and climate requirements so spreads the primrose.

The American Rhododendron Society reminds us that "over a thousand species, varying in size from tiny creepers to towering trees, offer exceptional variety to the gardener."

The Camellia is cultivated in a variety of climates in the United States, accepting winter temperatures as low as 10° (the hardiest varieties) and summer heat in the 100° range.

Joining a society is a way to greater enjoyment with plants and people.

One good reason for the formation of the many plant societies of America is the opportunity to share experiences; learning from others who have walked the path of discovery. Sharing experiences through plant societies comes with leaflets, bulletins, books, meetings and other activities and publications.

So, if any plant is special to you—why not join the plant society of its name. Here are a few of their addresses:

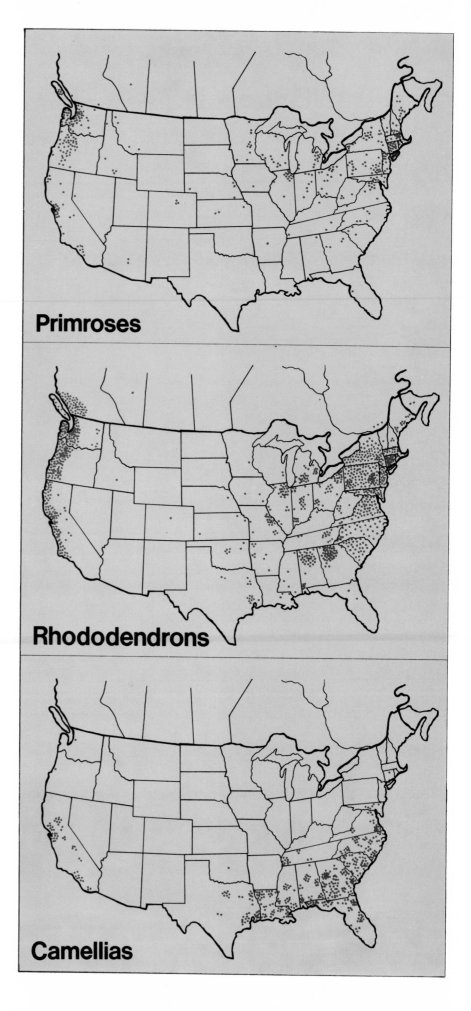

**Primroses**

**Rhododendrons**

**Camellias**

# Plant societies

### African Violet Society of America, Inc.

Box 1326, Knoxville, TN 37901
Membership $6.00 yearly includes "African Violet Magazine" 5 times per year.

### American Begonia Society

14050 Ramona Drive, Whittier, CA 90605.
Annual dues: $4.00. Monthly publication: "The Begonian."

### American Bonsai Society

229 North Shore Drive, Lake Waukomis, Parkville, MO 64151.
Annual dues: $10.00. Quarterly publication, "The Bonsai Journal."

### American Boxwood Society

Boyce, VA 22620.
Annual dues: $5.00. Quarterly publication: "The Boxwood Bulletin."

### American Camellia Society

Box 212, Fort Valley, GA 31030.
Dues: $7.50. Send for: "Camellias for Beginners," $1.15 ppd.

### American Daffodil Society

89 Chicherster Rd., New Canaan, CT 06840.
Annual dues: $5. Quarterly publication: "Daffodil Journal." Available to non-members: "The Daffodil Handbook," 240 pages, illus., $3.40 ppd.

### American Dahlia Society

163 Grant St., Dover, NJ 07801.
Annual dues: $6.00. Quarterly Bulletin and Annual Classification Book.

### American Fern Society

Dept. of Botany, Univ. of Rhode Island, Kingston, RI 02881.
Annual dues: $5.00. Quarterly publication: "American Fern Journal"; also quarterly Newsletter.

### American Fuchsia Society

1600 Prospect St., Belmont, CA 94002.
Annual dues: $4.00. Monthly publication: "Bulletin of the American Fuchsia Society."

### American Gloxinia & Gesneriad Society

Box 174, New Milford, CT 06776.
Annual dues: $5.00. Bi-monthly publication: "The Gloxinian."

### American Hemerocallis Society

Signal Mountain, TN 37377.
Annual dues: $5.00. Quarterly publication: "The Hemerocallis Journal."

### American Hibiscus Society

Box 98, Eagle Lake, FL 33839.
Annual dues: $5.00. Quarterly publication: "The Seed Pod."

*Iris*

### American Iris Society

Missouri Botanical Garden, 2315 Tower Grove Ave., St. Louis, MO 63110.
Annual dues: $7.50. Quarterly publication: "AIS Bulletin."

### American Magnolia Society

2150 Woodward Ave., Bloomfield Hills, MI 48013.
Annual dues: $5.00. Illustrated newsletters.

### American Orchid Society

Botanical Museum of Harvard Univ., Cambridge, MA 02138.
Annual dues: $12.50. Monthly publication: "American Orchid Society Bulletin."

### The American Plant Life Society and The American Amaryllis Society

Box 150, La Jolla, CA 92037.
Membership $5.00 per year includes "Plant Life—Amaryllis Yearbook" bulletin.

### The American Primrose Society

14015 84th Ave., NE Bothell, WA 98011.
Membership of $5.00 per year includes "Quarterly of the American Primrose Society."

### American Rhododendron Society

Secretary: Bernice J. Lamb, 2232 N.E. 78th Ave., Portland, OR 79213.
Annual dues: $10. Send for: "The Fundamentals of Rhododendron and Azalea Culture," 50¢.

### American Rock Garden Society

99 Pierpont Rd., Waterbury, CT 06705.
Annual dues: $5.00. Quarterly Bulletin.

### American Rose Society

4048 Poselea Pl., Columbus, OH 43214.
Annual dues: $10.50. Monthly publication: "American Rose"; "American Rose Annual."

### Bromeliad Society

Box 3279, Santa Monica, CA 90403.
Annual dues: $7.50. Bi-monthly publication: "Journal."

### Cactus and Succulent Society of America, Inc.

Box 167, Reseda, CA 91335.
Membership: $10.00 per year includes "Cactus and Succulent Journal" bi-monthly.

### Epiphyllum Society of America

218 E. Graystone Avenue., Monrovia, GA 91016.
Membership: $2.00 per year includes "Epiphyllum Bulletin," irregular.

### Herb Society of America

300 Massachusetts Ave., Boston, MA 02115.
Annual dues: $12.50. Annual publication: "The Herbalist."

### International Geranium Society

2547 Blvd. Del Campo, San Luis Obispo, CA 93401.
Annual dues: $4.00. Publication: "Geraniums Around the World."

*Hibiscus*

### National Oleander Society

5127 Ave. O-½, Galveston, TX 77550.
Annual dues: $5.00.

### The Indoor Light Gardening Society of America, Inc.

4 Wildwood Road, Greenville, SC 29607.
Membership: $5.00 per year includes "Light Garden" bi-monthly.

### The Palm Society

7229 SW 54th Avenue, Miami, FL 33143
Membership: $10.00 per year includes "Principes" quarterly.

### Saintpaulia International

Box 10604, Knoxville, TN 37914
Membership: $4.00 per year includes "Gesneriad Saintpaulia News" bi-monthly.

# Horticultural societies

## American Society for Horticultural Science

Box 109, St. Joseph, MI 49085.
Bi-monthly publications reports latest results in horticultural research.

## American Horticultural Society

910 N. Washington Street, Alexandria, VA 22314.
Membership: $15 per year, includes newsletter and quarterly magazine.
Local societies are established in many areas. A "Directory of American Horticulture" is available from the American Horticultural Society with listing of local groups.

## Garden clubs

### Garden Club of America

598 Madison Avenue, New York, NY 10022.

### National Council of State Garden Clubs, Inc.

4401 Magnolia Avenue
St. Louis, MO 63110.

### Men's Garden Clubs of America

5560 Merle Hay Road, Des Moines, IA 50323.
National offices will provide you with state or local group addresses.

## Horticultural magazines

### The Avant Gardener

Box 489, New York, NY 10028.
$10 per year for bi-weekly newsletter.
Latest information about horticulture.

### Flower and Garden

4251 Pennsylvania, Kansas City, MO 64111.
Monthly publication, $3 annually. Helpful gardening magazine; regionalized.

### Horticulture

300 Massachusetts Avenue, Boston, MA 02115.
Monthly magazine of Massachusetts Horticultural Society; $8 per year.

### Organic Gardening and Farming

Emmaus, PA 18099.
$6.85 per year for monthly magazine.

### Plants Alive

2100 North 45th, Seattle, WA 98102.
Magazine of indoor and greenhouse gardening; $9 per year; published monthly except July and August.

### Under Glass

Lord and Burnham, Box 114, Irvington, NY 10533.
Bi-monthly greenhouse information for $2.50 per year.

## Cooperative extension service

The Cooperative Extension Service is a storehouse of the latest "tried and true" localized information for the home gardener. As the name implies, the Cooperative Extension Service is a *cooperative* effort of the United States Department of Agriculture and each state university. The latest findings and developments in the field of agriculture, fruit and nut crops, and horticulture from the USDA and university cooperating experiment stations flows, where it applies locally, into the office of the *Cooperative* County Extension Service.

There are 3,150 Extension Service Offices across the country—one in practically every county. One of the aims of the County Extension Agent is to put the results and findings of all the experiments and trials in the hands of the home gardener, but *you* have to ask for it.

## What's in a name?

Unfortunately there isn't a standardized name for the "County Agent" or the "Cooperative Extension Service" used consistently throughout the states. If you don't know who your County Agent is, the key is to look in the phone book under the name of your county for the Cooperative Extension Service, or to check in the yellow pages under the County Government Offices. If all else fails, you can write to your state university and request a list of County Extension Offices; they'll be happy to furnish the information.

## The Extension Service changes

The change in the Extension Service is apparent in the changes being made in the names of the County Agent; the word *agriculture* is being phased out in the name. The County Extension Agent is no longer just a County Agriculture Agent. Before acres of farm and orchard land gave way to suburbia the name "Farm Advisor" fit the function of the agent very well. In counties where the small farm is alive and well, the "Farm Advisor" is still a good one, but in counties taken over by expanding cities, the farms change to home gardens and "gardens" in townhouses and high rise apartments.

For the home gardener this change means the campus of the state university has been extended to include interested gardeners everywhere. Not only the county office but the university can be an invaluable source of information on many subjects. On the following page we have listed the addresses of the state universities in the area. A letter to the office indicated of your state university, asking for a list of all available publications may bring you a surprisingly long list of bulletins, pamphlets and books.

For example, *Terrariums,* 32 page booklet. How to build various types; photographs and plant lists. Univ. of Illinois, C-1086, 50¢

*Foliage Plants for Interiors,* Rutgers University, New Jersey, Bulletin E-372-A. 50¢

*House Plants for Your Home,* one of Penn. State University's correspondence courses. This is an 11 lesson course covering the basics of house plant culture. NV 144. $6.00

*Care of House Plants,* Colorado State University's correspondence course of 9 lessons. Course 100. $2.50

## State Extension Service offices

AK: Coop. Ext. Svc., *Univ. of Alaska,* College AL 99701.

CT: Agricultural Publications, *Univ. of Connecticut,* Storrs CT 06268.

DE: Mailing Rm., Agricultural Hall, *Univ. of Delaware,* Newark DE 19711.

IL: Agricultural Publications Office, 123 Mumford Hall, *Univ. of Illinois,* Urbana IL 61801.

IN: Mailing Rm., Agricultural Admin. Bldg., *Purdue Univ.,* West Lafayette IN 47907.

IA: Publications Distribution Center, Printing and Publications Bldg., *Iowa State Univ.,* Ames IA 50010.

KS: Distribution Center, Umberger Hall, *Kansas State Univ.,* Manhattan KS 66502.

ME: Dept. of Public Information, PICS Bldg., *Univ. of Maine,* Orono ME 04473.

MA: Coop. Ext. Svc., Stockbridge Hall, *Univ. of Massachusetts,* Amherst MA 01002.

MI: MSU Bulletin Office, Box 231, *Michigan State Univ.,* East Lansing MI 48823.

MN: Bulletin Rm., Coffey Hall, *Univ. of Minnesota,* St. Paul MN 55101.

MO: Publications, B-9 Whitten Hall, *Univ. of Missouri,* Columbia MO 95201.

NB: Dept. of Information, Col. of Agriculture, *Univ. of Nebraska,* Lincoln NB 68503.

NH: Mail Svc., Hewitt Hall, *Univ. of New Hampshire,* Durham NH 03824.

NJ: Bulletin Clerk, Col. of Agriculture, *Rutgers Univ.,* New Brunswick NJ 08903.

NY: Mailing Rm., Bldg. 7, Research Park, *Cornell Univ.,* Ithaca NY 14850.

ND: Dept. of Agricultural Information, *North Dakota State Univ.,* Fargo ND 51802.

OH: Extension Office, *Ohio State Univ.,* 2120 Fyffe Rd., Columbus OH 43210.

PA: Sales Supervisor, 230 Ag. Admin. Bldg., *Pennsylvania State Univ.,* University Park PA 16802.

RI: Resource Information Office, 16 Woodward Hall, *Univ. of Rhode Island,* Kingston RI 02881.

SD: Agricultural Information Office, Extension Bldg., *South Dakota State Univ.,* Brookings SD 57006.

VT: Publications Office, Morrill Hall, *Univ. of Vermont,* Burlington VT 05401.

WI: Agricultural Bulletin Bldg., 1535 Observatory Dr., *Univ. of Wisconsin,* Madison WI 53706.

# Government publications

Home gardeners everywhere also have a voluminous source of information in the United States government publications. To get acquainted with the available material write, Superintendent of Documents, Government Printing Office, Washington, D.C. for:

*List of Available Publications of the U.S.D.A.,*
Bulletin No. 11, 45¢.

Below is a sample of their publications:

*Minigardens for Vegetables,*
Home & Garden Bulletin No. 163, 15¢.

*Growing Vegetables in the Home Garden,*
Home & Garden Bulletin No. 202, 75¢.

*Home Propagation of Ornamental Trees and Shrubs,*
Home & Garden Bulletin No. 80, 10¢.

*Indoor Gardens with Controlled Lighting,*
Home & Garden Bulletin No. 187, 15¢.

*Selecting and Growing House Plants,*
Home & Garden Bulletin No. 82, 15¢.

*Plant Hardiness and Zone Map,*
Miscellaneous Publication No. 814, 25¢.

The city and suburban gardener should not expect a person to person interview when calling on the services of the County Extension Agent. The *office* of the County Extension Agent is the source of information. The Cooperative Extension Service is finding new ways to reach more home gardeners. Some Extension Services have even started a telephone information service—"Dial-a-Home & Garden Tip"—a one minute recorded message which give information of current interest to the home gardener.

In many areas the Extension Service has magnified its range by means of radio and newspaper coverage, as well as issuing monthly bulletins and newsletters. In some areas the Cooperative Extension Service sponsors monthly, informal classes on various phases of gardening, and in other counties the Extension Service has played an important part in establishing community gardens.

# Landscape architects

These highly trained specialists can help solve your problems with altering the climate on your property. Check the yellow page listings for your area to locate landscape architects or write to:

**American Society of Landscape Architects**
1750 Old Meadow Road
McLean, VA 22101.

The national organization can help you locate nearby specialists and provide you with information, including a quarterly publication "Landscape Architecture."

An excellent booklet has been published by the American Society of Landscape Architects Foundation in conjunction with the U.S. Department of the Interior, National Park Service, entitled "Plants/People/and Environmental Quality." Order from Superintendent of Documents, U.S. Government Printing Office, Washington, DC 20402. Price $4.

# Special library collections

Here are some outstanding horticultural libraries. Most are open to the public for reference work.

DISTRICT OF COLUMBIA

**Smithsonian Institution Libraries**
Natural History Building
Washington, DC 20560

**U.S. National Arboretum Library**
Washington, DC 20002

ILLINOIS

**Chicago Horticultural Society Library**
Botanic Garden, P. O. Box 90
Glencoe, IL 60022

MASSACHUSETTS

**Arnold Arboretum, Harvard University**
22 Divinity Avenue
Cambridge, MA 02318

**Massachusetts Horticultural Society**
300 Massachusetts Avenue
Boston, MA 02115

MICHIGAN

**Michigan Horticultural Society**
The White House, Belle Isle
Detroit, MI 48207

MINNESOTA

**University of Minnesota**
St. Paul Campus Library
St. Paul, MN 55101

MISSOURI

**Missouri Botanical Garden Library**
2315 Tower Grove Avenue
St. Louis, MO 63108

NEBRASKA

**University of Nebraska, East Campus**
C. Y. Thompson Library
Lincoln, NE 68503

NEW HAMPSHIRE

**University of New Hampshire**
Biological Sciences Library
Kendall Hall
Durham, NH 03824

NEW JERSEY

**Rutgers University**
Cook College, Box 231
New Brunswick, NJ 08903

NEW YORK

**Brooklyn Botanic Garden Library**
1000 Washington Avenue
Brooklyn, NY 11225

**Cornell University**
Albert R. Mann Library
Ithaca, NY 14850

**New York Botanical Garden Library**
Bronx, NY 10458

**The Horticultural Society of New York**
128 West 58th Street
New York, NY 10019

OHIO

**Ohio Agricultural Research and Development Center Library**
Wooster, OH 44691

**The Garden Center of Greater Cleveland**
Eleanor Squire Library
11030 East Boulevard
Cleveland, OH 44106

PENNSYLVANIA

**The Morris Arboretum**
University of Pennsylvania
9414 Meadowbrook Avenue
Philadelphia, PA 19118

**Pennsylvania State University**
Agricultural and Biological Sciences Library
University Park, PA 16802

**The Pennsylvania Horticultural Society, Inc.**
325 Walnut Street
Philadelphia, PA 19106

SOUTH DAKOTA

**South Dakota State University**
Lincoln Memorial Library
Brookings, SD 57006

CANADA

**Civic Garden Centre Library**
Metro Toronto Edwards Gardens
777 Lawrence Avenue, East
Don Mills, Ontario, Canada M3C 1P2

**Royal Botanical Gardens**
Box 399
Hamilton, Ontario, Canada L8N 3H8

# Arboretums and botanical gardens

Professional horticultural centers are excellent sources of help for the home gardener. Many have publications available at minimal costs. Some offer educational classes and others welcome volunteer gardeners for experimentation. Most have information services to answer your questions.

CONNECTICUT

**Bartlett Arboretum of the State of Connecticut**
151 Brookdale Road, Stamford, CT 06903

DISTRICT OF COLUMBIA

**U.S. National Arboretum**
Washington, DC 20002

**U. S. Botanical Garden Conservatory**
Maryland Avenue and 1st Streets, SW
Washington, DC 20024

IOWA

**University of Northern Iowa**
Cedar Falls, IA 50613

ILLINOIS

**Botanic Garden of the Chicago Horticultural Society**
775 Dundee Road, Box 90
Glencoe, IL 60022

**Lincoln Park Conservatory**
2400 North Stockton Drive
Chicago, IL 60614

INDIANA

**Christy Woods Arboretum**
Ball State University, Muncie, IN 47302

KANSAS

**Meade Park Garden Center**
124 North Fillmore, Topeka, KS 66606

**The Bartlett Arboretum**
Belle Plaine, KS 67013

MASSACHUSETTS

**Alexandra Botanic Garden and Hunnewell Arboretum**
Wellesley College, Wellesley, MA 02181

**Botanic Garden of Smith College**
Northampton, MA 01060

MAINE

**Fay Hyland Botanical Plantation**
317 Deering Hall, University of Maine
Orono, ME 04473

MICHIGAN

**Anna Scripps Whitcomb Conservatory**
Belle Isle, Detroit, MI 48207

**Beal-Garfield Botanic Garden**
Michigan State University
East Lansing, MI 48823

**Nichols Arboretum**
University of Michigan
Ann Arbor, MI 48104

MINNESOTA

**Botanical Garden of the University of Minnesota**
St. Paul, MN 55101

MISSOURI

**Missouri Botanical Garden**
2315 Tower Grove Avenue
St. Louis, MO 63110

NEW JERSEY

**Rutgers Display Gardens**
Rutgers University
New Brunswick, NJ 08903

NEW YORK

**Brooklyn Botanic Garden**
1000 Washington Avenue
Brooklyn, NY 11225

**L. H. Bailey Hortorium**
Mann Hall, Cornell University
Ithaca, NY 14850

**New York Botanical Garden**
Bronx Park, Bronx, NY 10458

**Queens Botanical Garden**
43-50 Main Street, Flushing, NY 11355

OHIO

**Cox Arboretum**
6733 Springboro Pike, Dayton, OH 45449

**Garden Center of Greater Cincinnati**
2715 Reading Road
Cincinnati, OH 45206

**The Garden Center of Greater Cleveland**
11030 East Boulevard
Cleveland, OH 44106

PENNSYLVANIA

**Longwood Gardens**
Kennett Square, PA 19348

**Pittsburgh Garden Center**
1059 Shady Ave., Pittsburgh, PA 15232

**The Morris Arboretum**
University of Pennsylvania
9414 Meadowbrook Avenue
Philadelphia, PA 19118

WISCONSIN

**University of Wisconsin Arboretum**
1207 Seminole Highway
Madison, WI 53711

CANADA

**Botanic Garden and Field Laboratory**
University of Alberta
Edmonton, Alberta, Canada

**Botanical Garden**
University of British Columbia
Vancouver, B.C., Canada V6T 1W5

**Montreal Botanical Garden**
4101 Sherbrooke Street, East
Montreal, Quebec, Canada

**Royal Botanical Gardens**
Box 399
Hamilton, Ontario, Canada L8N 3H8